MYSTERY TO MASTERY SERIES

Forex
Trading

JOSE BLASCO & BECKY HAYMAN

Printed in the United States of America

ISBN: 978-1-956019-57-5 (paperback)

ISBN: 978-1-956019-58-2 (ebook)

tradewithufos

traddictiv®

TRADDICTIV PTE. LTD.

Singapore

CONTENTS

Resources

With the purchase of this book, you have unlocked a free Forex course, as well as free access to our AutoClimate™ and AutoUFOs® apps for TradingView for 3 months:

To claim your free Forex course and apps, go to www.tradewithufos.com/redeem

Learning to trade an asset class alone can be difficult and overwhelming. We're here to help you with whatever tools make the most sense for you:

Apps

Apart from using our apps to increase precision trading, AutoClimate™ and AutoUFOs® can be a useful time-saving tool during the learning process, especially when combined with the market replay functionality available in TradingView.

Three links to remember:

Unlocking your free Forex course automatically grants you access to the AutoClimate™ and AutoUFOs® apps for TradingView. www.tradewithufos.com/redeem

TradingView offers a free plan as well as paid memberships (our app works perfectly with their free plan). Start your own TradingView account here:
www.tradewithufos.com/tradingview

Explore other trading apps, such as the MetaTrader apps, right here:
www.tradewithufos.com/apps

Coaching

The knowledge acquired by reading this book provides a great foundation. In general, we cannot do much without knowledge – congratulations for being open to educating yourself!

Having said that, experience proves that knowledge is step one, which should be followed by step two, which is skill building through practice. Here are additional free resources to eliminate bad habits that come from isolation and help transform your knowledge into a powerful skill:

Attend live trading and coaching sessions. Interact with your coach and other traders. Ask questions. www.tradewithufos.com/coaching

Watch recorded trading and coaching sessions to save time and speed up your development:
www.youtube.com/c/tradewithufos

Additional Courses

One of the risks attached to trading is falling in love with trading, as many of us do. Now that you have learned a lot about Forex trading, you may realize that you'd like to work further on your trading plan, maybe you'd prefer to refine your methodology using back-testing techniques, or you now understand the impact of trading emotions and you'd like to work further on mastering the trader in you, or you'd simply like to learn to trade other assets, such as stocks, options, futures or digital/crypto assets.

To help you understand your education choices further go to: www.tradewithufos.com/courses

FAQ

We expect you to have questions while going through the process of learning how to trade or working to improve your current skillset. If you have any questions, please feel free to use the Q&A section on our website. You can also connect with Jose and Becky there: www.tradewithufos.com/questions

Social Media and Contact

We are online and we love interaction!

Please find us on your favorite social media network, or use our support email: support@traddictiv.com

Our social media channels are all here: https://linktr.ee/tradewithufos

We would truly appreciate if you could follow/like us – and, most importantly, share the word with the world! Many people may be able to use our help. They just need to know we exist ☺

Thank you for reading us!

INTRODUCTION

This book is written by traders, for traders.

We love the financial markets and all they can do for us. In this book, we will focus on the Forex markets in particular. We're going to discuss them from all angles. We will start from the foundation, which is, of course, critical and extremely important. From that base, we will build our specific methodology on how to enter and exit the market, with specific rules covering everything you need to know when trading:

- When to buy (and at what price)
- When to sell (and at what price)
- When not to trade at all
- Where to get out of the trade
- Which currency to trade
- What position size to use
- How to manage risk

The rules will be clearly defined, but the rest is up to you. We count on your discipline, and that you will apply these lessons the way they are suggested. As traders, if we want consistent results, we must exhibit consistent action. Bending the rules, or not having any rules at all, leads to random action, which produces random results. Can random action lead to profit? Yes, but that would mainly be down to luck. Our approach is not about luck, but relying on our specific trading plan.

We will explore the theory behind what we do and then dive into the use of technology, which is key, as these are the tools we use to trade as professionally and objectively as possible.

The content of this book will provide you with knowledge about trading and a specific methodology but, what is very important, is transferring knowledge into skill. The way we do that, as human beings, is through practice, so we recommend that you practice the application of the concepts, from basic to more advanced, as you go through the content.

However, what you'll notice as you go through the book is that one of the most important elements of trading successfully is trading psychology. No matter the methodology, no matter the technology, no matter how much practice, if you don't manage your own emotions, you will run into big problems in your trading. Some people argue that psychology is 99% of trading. Although we are not psychologists, and the specific percentage of the impact of psychology on trading could be debated, what we all know for sure is that it is human beings clicking the button. For that reason, the often-overlooked element of trading psychology will feature heavily in our plans.

Ultimately, our goal is to end up with a set of rules that help traders act mechanically.

LOOKING FOR BALANCE

The classical way that people learn to trade is to first look at a chart and try to understand the basics of what that chart is and go from there to learn different strategies. We would like you to think about trading from a much more professional standpoint and first think about mindset, before getting into methodology. If you have a balanced mindset, and then add a proper methodology, you are more likely to be in a good place with your trading. If you master an amazing methodology but don't have the balanced mindset, you will very likely get in trouble because of the impact of emotions.

In trading, there are three key factors that define the quality of a trade or investment. We need to find a balance between those:

- Probability that the trade will win
- Achievable reward
- Risk

One thing in the market that is guaranteed (and we won't use that word very often when talking about trading) is that you will have losing trades. There is no strategy that can gain profits 100% of the time. That's just part of trading. The balance of the risk against reward and probability is what helps us manage this over time.

This might seem like common sense, especially for those who may have been in business before or traded before. Of course, we want to say that we'll execute trades in markets where we will gain more when we're right than what we could lose if we're wrong, as well as having probability that we'll be right more often than being wrong. However, this is not the way that most people approach the markets; usually, people give priority to one of those three factors and just go for that. There are some who chase high probability, meaning they want to be right or have winning trades 95% of the time, but don't pay much attention to their risk or reward. They may be right most of the time, which is nice, but when they're wrong, which is almost never, they can lose badly and wipe out a majority of their gains. This then means having to execute dozens of additional trades just to get the account back to breakeven, and so on. In this case you can see that not losing often, but being badly hurt by unprofitable trades, is not a well-balanced situation.

Jose's background prior to trading was as an engineer, so his mindset was to focus on perfection. When he started learning about trading strategies that were right less than 80% of the time, he believed that to be the sign of a weak trader. He realized over time that this is absolutely not the case. You can be right 80% of the time with small winners and be okay, and lose 20% of the time with big losses and end up not doing very well. On the other hand, you can actually trade in such a way where you can be wrong more than you're right; maybe you win 40% of the time, but the size of your profits is great and the size of your losses are small so overall you may still be profitable, despite being wrong more often. It's easy to fall in the trap of trying to be a perfectionist but, in the markets, we don't need to be.

If you shoot for rewards that are decent yet achievable, you don't need to shoot for the trade of the year, which, by definition, only happens once a year, and we never know when that will be!

Trading is not about winning all the time. It's also not about losing a lot, either, while hoping to get the really big winners. It's all about balance; finding the sweet spot. It's helpful to use ratios to understand what this sweet spot is:

- Win/Loss Ratio = the number of winners out of the trades you've taken. For example, if you have a win/loss ratio of 70%, then 70% of your trades have been profitable and 30% of your trades lost
- Average* Reward-to-Risk Ratio = the average profit you make when you're right versus the average loss you take when you're wrong

*Notice the word "average." This is not just about the profit you make when you're right versus the loss you take when you're wrong. There are many trading books that will explain these kinds of ratios. Often, traders have a fixed reward-to-risk ratio. Let's say that someone decides to go for a 5:1 reward-to-risk ratio. For every $100 they risk, they stand to gain $500. They risk five times less than what they could gain on a trade.

While this sounds great, it doesn't take into consideration something quite fundamental about the markets: They change. Maybe a market is more volatile, or less volatile, over time. Maybe those kinds of reward-to-risk trades only happen under certain circumstances. It's not every day the market provides us with opportunities to catch a 5:1 move.

To be able to create consistent results means we want to have methodologies that allow us to trade through changing marketplace conditions, so we can be adaptable as traders. A much more interesting way to measure the quality of the methodology is not by looking at it one trade at a time, but to analyze it after a collection of trades to evaluate your average reward-to-risk ratio. Some hit 4:1, some 3:1, some 8:1, some break even, where you took profits based on different conditions and circumstances. Some of the trades will have lost, too. Overall, you'll be able to see what your average risk-to-reward ratio is.

Something we will explain later in more depth is that you will need a minimum of 30 trades to have enough sample data to analyze how well your methodology is working. Analyzing results after five trades is nowhere near enough to see any trends in your data. Ideally, you'd have at least 100 trades, but 30 is an absolute minimum.

Once you have your average reward-risk ratio, you multiply that by your win-loss ratio to see what to expect from your methodology and what it is capable of producing for you through time, over changing market conditions.

The reason this is so important is that if you don't know what to expect from your methodology, how can you help yourself to manage your emotions?

The key when trading is to be balanced so you can be more in control, managing your emotions so you feel trading is effortless, and be in the state of mind where trading is peaceful. You need to be calm and be able to understand what's going on and what you have in front of you. There's no way you can do that unless you know your expectation.

This is a critical element of trading, and many people fail to understand or realize it early on in their trading journey or trading education. An example of trading without first having an expectation: You buy a trading book with a great methodology on how to trade. You finish the book and understand all the steps you need to take to execute the methodology, but you have no idea how much you could make with that methodology because you have never executed it before – you just know how it works because you read about it. You don't know what to expect because you've never done it before. Now let's say you implement that methodology, and the first three trades you take are winners. How can you avoid getting euphoric? Let's say the first three trades are losses. How can you avoid becoming fearful and maybe giving up on the methodology entirely?

Maybe if you'd have kept going to 30 trades or more, you would be overall in profit. But you're more likely to give up after three losses because you became fearful – and because you didn't know what to expect.

The same is true if you want to build any business, and trading is a business. If you wanted to start a restaurant business and didn't know how many customers you could expect per day in different neighborhoods, how would you know where to open your first restaurant? If you chose a location at random, then you wouldn't be acting like a businessperson, but depending on luck. We need to move away from that as businesspeople and as traders. If you were to collect a nice sample of trades and understand what your expectation is, then – and only then – will you begin to trade with real capital, and be in a much more likely position to do a good job.

Here is the formula to calculate expectation (assuming that the trader always risks the same amount of capital per trade):

$$^{***} Expectation = \left(\frac{Win}{Loss} Ratio \times AvgRRR \right) - \frac{Loss}{Win} Ratio$$

Let's do an example:

- Resulting Win/Loss Ratio = 48%
- Resulting Average Reward-to-Risk Ratio = 2.1 = AvgRRR
- Resulting Expectation = (0.48 x 2.1) – 0.52 = 0.488

Once you have your expectation of both win-loss ratio and reward-to-risk ratio, and you also understand the average amount of trades you could take that fit the methodology, you can start to analyze this against your goals. Taking the example above, let's say the trader now wants to know more about how much can be made with this methodology if 89 trades were taken in one year with a 1% risk rule:

- Trades per year x expectation x risk rule %
- 89 x 0.488 x 1% = 43.432% (annual return)

This example assumes 89 trades are taken in a year. There are 252 trading days in a year, so this would mean about two or three trades a week were taken. Of course, if someone trades a different style where they trade more or less than this example, or if their expectation figures are different, then the expected outcome in terms of yearly return could vary by quite a lot.

This example also assumes a 1% risk rule. We will cover this properly later, but a classical rule in the industry (which is a very healthy rule) is to define the amount of money you are willing to pay per trade to see what happens next. This is the definition of risk. Let's say you are comfortable with going to the movie theater and paying "x" amount of dollars to watch a movie. Your risk is a potential waste of your time and those dollars. That is what you are willing to pay to see what happens next, even if you get nothing from it. What's your reward? To watch the movie of the century and have the time of your life. Thus, your risk is weighed up against your reward.

Let's say you are willing to risk $20 on a trade to see what happens next. Potentially, you came up with twenty because your account is $4,000 and you decided to risk 0.5% of your account. This number will be different per trader and there are different ways to arrive at this number, but in this instance, we'll use a 0.5% risk rule. Let's also assume that, from gathered data, the trader expects a Win/Loss Ratio of 46%, an average

17

reward-to-risk ratio of 2.6 and assumes to take 112 trades per year. This is how they would calculate their expected yearly gain:

- Risk Rule = 0.5%
- Resulting Win/Loss Ratio = 46%
- Resulting Average Reward-to-Risk Ratio = 2.6 = AvgRRR
- Resulting Expectation = (0.46 x 2.6) – 0.54 = 0.656
- Trades per year = 112
- 112 x 0.656 x 0.5% = 36.736% Annual Return

Once we do these calculations, we can see if our strategy works for the goals we have, if there are some parameters we might need to change, or if we need to change our idea about what is realistic. In the above examples, we would know that 43% per year or 36% per year, respectively, are not crazy numbers to aim for.

If you don't know what to expect by taking a little bit of time to learn how to trade properly, and collecting data samples and analyzing the results, it could be that you overestimate or underestimate what is realistic for you. Maybe you trade five times in a month and four are winners and one is a loser. You might say "that's great, I'm doing really well," or you might say the opposite and assume you've not done as well as you could, only because you don't, actually, know what is realistic with the methodology that you are applying.

We need to base our goals on something more tangible, as it makes it easier to maintain our balanced mindset as we progress with our trading. This is why putting some effort into the above process is really helpful. Approaching trading as a business means needing to be committed, which is much easier if your mindset is healthy when trading and going through the runs of profits and losses.

This will not be a process that is done once in your life and that's it. It is a healthy process that ideally is repeated from time to time, especially when trying out new methodologies or new markets.

When you start, it is advisable to start with a paper money account (also called a "simulated" or "demo" account) to practice and gather your data, or at least use a small amount of money with a low-risk percentage per trade. As you progress and you've been trading for a while – and you're comfortable risking real or more money – you will keep monitoring your results to see if they match your expectations. If you have deviations, you will then analyze your data to see what you can learn from it (we will discuss reviewing trades later on).

TOOLS OF A TRADER

When it comes to trading, there are two elements: planning and execution. When we refer to the tools of a trader, we are usually referring to the technological tools used to help us with both of these elements.

BROKERS AND PLATFORMS

Firstly, we need a broker and a trading platform. These often come together, but not always.

A **broker** is the company who sends your buy and sell orders to the exchange or interbank market. Say, for example, you want to buy a US stock; your stockbroker will route your order to an exchange such as the New York Stock Exchange (NYSE). Essentially, your broker sends your order to be executed. There are online brokers, as well as brokers that you could call to place orders.

A **platform** is the software that you use to view charts, see the matrix of price, use indicators, etc. It is either web-based or a downloadable software and it allows you to view market data.

Market data is important for many types of people to be able to see, not just traders: maybe market analysts, finance analysts or businesses who need to buy a lot of a commodity, such as cocoa or oil. As traders, our trading platform is our bread and butter because this is what gives us the tools to analyze and plan our trades.

Brokers often have their own platforms, so you can view a chart, make a decision on your trade or place a buy or sell order directly onto the platform, and the broker routes it through to the exchange, all in one. However, there are also situations where you have a brokerage that does not have an online platform or a platform that is not a broker. You might see platforms where you can see charts and price data, but can't place a trade, or you can choose from a list of brokers to route your order through.

Whether your platform and broker are combined or not, you will need both: the ability to see price data and charts, and the ability to place an order that is routed to the exchange.

Different brokers and platforms charge different amounts and have different features, so it's always recommended to do some homework and find the one (or ones) that make the most sense for you.

We will be sharing snapshots throughout this book taken from the following applications:

TradingView (an independent platform linkable to various brokers):

MetaTrader (a.k.a. MT5, the newest version of a very popular platform used by many FX brokers):

MT5 - the mobile version (a generic opensource platform used by many FX brokers):

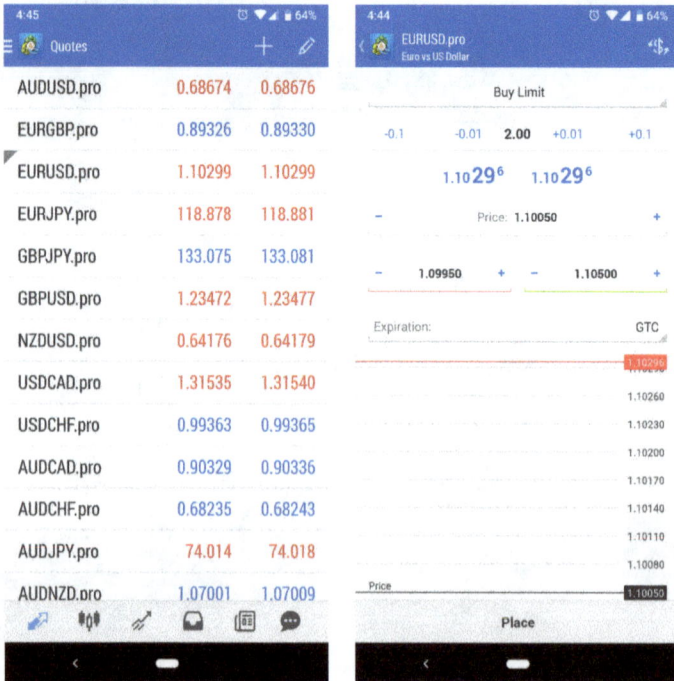

Most platforms have a desktop or web-based version, as well as a smartphone app version. We would usually suggest that the planning phase is done on as big a screen as possible, to lower the probability of making mistakes in your analysis. Execution can be done on your smartphone.

The reason we suggest this is that it helps to separate the two operations in your mind. One device is used for planning and one is used for execution. It can relieve the temptation of seeing the buy or the sell button on your bigger screen and wanting to press it to jump into a move that you see on the chart, feeling like you might be missing out. To keep ourselves under control a bit more easily, we separate the two functions using different devices and/or software.

Of course, you may use your computer for both planning and execution and use one platform for your planning and another platform (linked to a broker) to execute or, maybe, you prefer to plan and execute using the same device and the same platform. Ultimately, it is up to you – and the longer you trade, the more you will come to your own preferences. But if you are a beginner, we would recommend having some kind of system that separates planning from execution.

The good thing is, once you've used one platform, you've effectively used them all. They may have buttons in different places or look a bit different, but changing a timeframe is changing a timeframe; drawing a line is drawing a line, so, it's not like having to start from scratch to learn a new platform if you're already used to one.

TRADING EXECUTION TOOLS

Once a trade has been planned, it is time to execute. Execution involves multiple steps:

- Placing the initial order (your buy or sell order to enter the trade)
- Target placement (where you will get out of the trade if you were to profit)

The use of multiple targets or scaling out is a normal practice. Let's say you purchase 200 shares of a stock at a particular price, expecting the price to go up. Your final target is quite far away to the upside, and although you believe it could get there, it may not reach your target before falling again. The further away your target is, the less likely you are to reach it so, maybe, if the stock price reaches somewhere between your entry and your final target, you sell 100 shares. That way, you've collected some profits but are still in the trade with the remaining 100 shares.

- Stop losses (where you will get out of the trade if you were to be wrong)

Stop loss orders are imperative. We always, always, always use stops. We always, always, always use stops. One more time: We always, always, always use stops. Stop loss orders are programmed orders that take you out of a losing position automatically, even if you are not watching your screen or have no access to your trading platforms. Let's say you have a trade on but you're in the middle of something and cannot log in to your account. If something goes against you in the markets, your trading position will be closed for a predefined loss that you had preset before the market moved against you.

Even though it's not nice to be "stopped out" from a purely human point of view (we don't like losing), stop losses are something that we really appreciate. When we get stopped out, we know that we acted as professionals, following our plan and getting out when we said we would if the market was to move against us. On top of this, the automatic order happened at the speed of light, with perfect execution and no procrastination.

By using these stop loss orders, you are minimizing the amount of pain the market can give you if it behaves unexpectedly. Of course, it's not fun to lose, but it's part of the game and it's critical that you manage those losses. If not, you could end up with such a large loss that you may have to trade for six months just to make the money back, or have one large loss wipe out a huge chunk from your account.

It can get worse when trading markets like Forex, which use leverage. Leverage is different in different countries and from broker to broker, but let's say as an example your leverage is 50:1. If you don't use stop losses and the market goes against you, not only are you losing, but you are losing 50 times faster than if you weren't using leverage. Without stop losses, this can result in getting a margin call from your broker, and you may have lost all of your funds.

It is easy to avoid this: Use a stop loss! Simply click a button to give yourself some protection. We love stop losses. We always, always, always use stop losses.

Something which can cause concern about the use of stop loss orders is the practice amongst some brokers to look for traders' stops and manipulate price to hit them. This exercise of "chasing stops" is common, not only in Forex markets and decentralized interbank markets, but also in exchange-traded products. We need to be aware that the only way to profit is if someone else loses. This may not be a nice thing to hear, but it is a fact that brokers and market-makers know so, sometimes, they move price to reach stops, then add their size to a position to push the market in the way they wanted it to go anyway. There are those who would argue that using stop losses doesn't work because of this practice.

However, what if other traders' stops were our entries? If you've been trading before and been stopped out many times, only to see price turn just after, you may conclude that it is stop loss orders that are hurting you. But what if your entry was located where your stop was? In other words, if you were more precise on your entries, your stop losses would not hurt you, but help with risk management. You would be less likely to get stopped out because your entries would be in a better place.

Brokers do not move price against individuals, they move price in general, to where it is common for a lot of traders to have their stops. Common trading knowledge, gathered from the internet, books, etc., teaches the masses where to place stops and may have a lot of traders placing their stops in the same places on the charts. For example, placing a stop under a doji candle, above a resistance line, or below a support line.

In this book, you will see that we will be using trading technology to be more specific on our entries, and therefore we'll be using stops that will work to make us safer, not to make us magnets for brokers to stop us out. Our attempt will be to buy when the large players buy and to sell when the large players sell. In other words, we will be buying stops from other retail traders because we'll be buying when the large players buy, and vice versa.

Trading is not about always avoiding losses; it's about knowing how to lose when it is time to lose. This is done professionally, without getting emotional. You need to learn how to lose money correctly, meaning you have to be okay with losing a small amount. If you aren't, you will lose a lot of money because you didn't use a stop order to protect yourself. You need to learn how to lose money before you can make money. Trading cannot be a game where we are right all the time and be profitable on 100% of our trades.

If you want to avoid any, and all, losses it is better that you don't trade. If you want to make profits, you have to accept and embrace the risk of loss.

The great thing about markets like Forex is that using position sizing (which we will cover later on), you can determine and adjust the size of your risk, making the potential loss whatever size you choose. One of our earlier examples references 0.5% risk-per-trade, so 0.5% of your total trading account is at risk for each trade. Then you can work out on your platform almost exactly the amount of money that equates to and size your risk accordingly.

It's like if you start a company; you know you need customers to come to you. You accept that you will have customers who come to you and don't purchase anything, but the more unique you are and the more amazing and helpful your product is, the more likely it is that customers will come to you and stay with you.

Trading is also a business and we must be unique in this industry too. If we have a unique way to enter and exit markets, we have a higher chance of profit and a smaller chance of loss, but we still accept that loss will be a part of our business.

Long story short: We always, always, always use stops!

Monitoring/Cancelling/Replacing orders is also very common

This refers to trade management; being able to edit our trades once we've placed them, helps ensure we're always on top of what we're doing, updating our execution to the market conditions and environments that we find ourselves in.

Different execution tools apply depending on how active or visual a trader likes to be:

- You can execute straight from your phone or tablet
- You can execute from the charts themselves
- You can use what is known as the DOM (the depth of market)

As well as having slightly different ways of executing, different platforms have slightly different layouts when it comes to the same execution tools. Like most technology platforms, they perform the same functions and are very similar; we just have to get used to the layout.

In the below examples, we can see the layout for Bracket Execution using two different platforms. A Bracket Execution simply means placing a trade that has a stop and target attached to it. When placing our orders, it is helpful to use tools that allow us to send complete trades, so we don't forget to add a stop or add our target later.

The following images are showing order placements using MT5, MT5 mobile and TradingView, respectively. All show a demonstration of placing a bracket buy order: an order to buy with a stop loss to sell and a target to sell. We will cover order types later; this is simply to show how different platforms vary on layout with placing orders, but still allow us to enter the same information:

MT5:

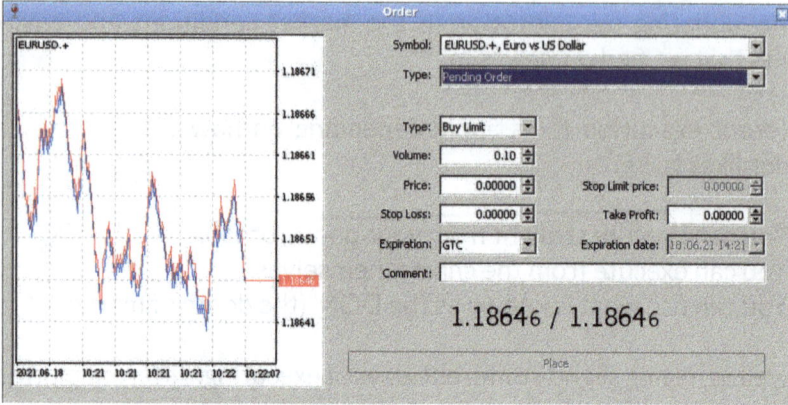

MT5 Mobile (left) and Trading View (right):

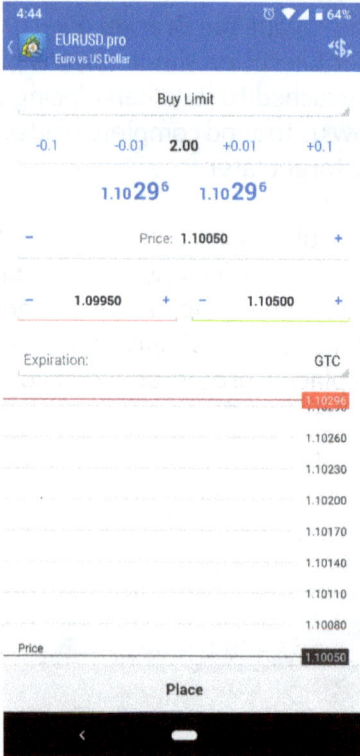

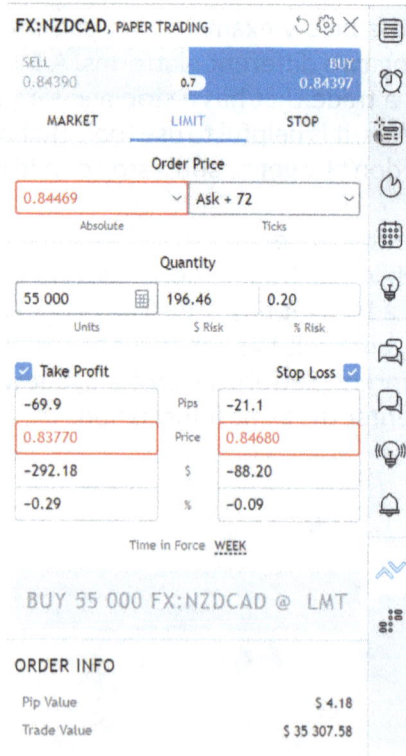

There is another type of execution tool called DOM (short for depth of market.) The DOM execution tool is like a ladder where you place your orders by clicking on the price itself and you can drag your orders along the ladder:

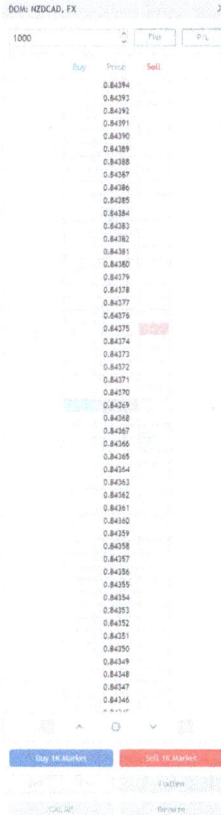

Market Data

Market data comes from either exchanges or other private sources of data. Markets like Futures, Options and Stocks are centralized, meaning that if you trade US stocks, for example, orders could be executed in the New York Stock Exchange, which is in a specific city in a specific country. If you trade British stocks, the execution would take place in the

London Stock Exchange; if you trade Japanese stocks, the execution will take place in the Tokyo Stock Exchange, and so on. When data is coming from an exchange, then the quality and authenticity of that data is very strong, as it's coming from the same place.

The decentralized nature of markets like Forex and cryptocurrencies means there is no exchange. With Forex, for instance, the execution happens in a bank, which could be located in Asia, Europe, the United States or anywhere in the world. It is an interbank system, not based in one central place. The job of our Forex broker is to act as a router, sending our orders to the bank that gives us a fill at the best price.

Some brokers do a better job than others at routing, so we want to make sure we use brokers that do a good job at routing to the best price. Therefore, the quality of the data that you get when trading decentralized products may, very much, depend on the quality of your broker.

Within Forex brokers, we'd normally find two types of accounts: those that charge a commission for the trades (these are usually the professional accounts) and those that allow you to trade commission-free, but offer worse rates (in other words, the commission is "free" but is built into the price). Either way, we are paying something, and that's the way it needs to be; they wouldn't route our orders for us if they weren't earning money somewhere so we have no problem paying some kind of commission. However, at the same time, we do need to be sensitive to using the right brokers with the right accounts. We always want to be trading where we are mimicking those large market players.

Oftentimes, brokers will offer you a choice of type of account, and the difference is usually the presence of commissions and how wide the spreads are. The professional accounts will be the ones that offer tighter spreads and will often charge a small commission. The non-professional accounts will be those that offer "no commission," but you'll see that the spreads are wider, meaning you are getting worse prices.

The platforms we use to trade need to be connected to real-time data. This means that the data we're seeing is current and up to date. Delayed data can be anywhere from 10 to 30 minutes behind the true and current price. We need real-time data feeds to spot the right price in which to execute our trade, or we could be late to a move. That does not give us an edge, and in the markets, we always need our edge.

Usually, real-time data coming from exchanges is chargeable, unless the broker you use waives such a fee. In such case, the exchange still charges for the real-time data, but such brokers waive it for their customers. This is rare; nearly all brokers will tend to charge a real-time data fee.

But real-time data from Forex brokers is often free because Forex is a decentralized product. This also applies to other markets like CFDs and cryptocurrencies. Some platforms, like TradingView, give you access to see many different markets; they will show you real-time data, in some cases, and delayed data in others, depending on the exchanges they are using. Be aware of the ones that are delayed – and understand that you may need to pay a fee to access the real-time data for these markets.

PRICE CHARTS

Charts are our bread and butter as traders. We use them to help us with nearly every aspect of our analysis. We will use them to identify whether or not we should be trading and, if so, when to enter and exit trades.

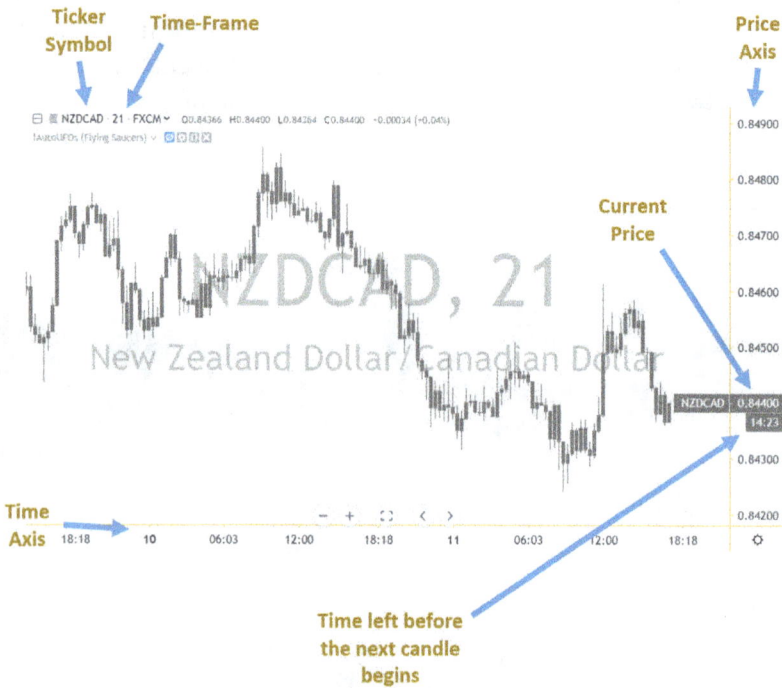

On any chart, we have a horizontal axis that shows you time and a vertical axis that shows you price, so each chart is simply the data of what price did over a period of time.

On the right-hand side, highlighted on the price axis (vertical axis), you will see whatever the current price is of the market you are looking at. This will be a number that moves in real-time (if you have real-time data).

It can also be handy to have a counter that shows you the time left before the next candle begins so, in the example above, we are looking at a 21-minute candle. At the end of each 21-minute period a new candle will form, which will show us new information.

Nearly all platforms allow you to customize your charts to change the colors and layouts to suit your visual preferences. You can change the color of the background, the numerical information on the chart, the candles, etc.

TICKER SYMBOLS

Usually, on the top left-hand side of the chart, we will see what is known as the "ticker symbol." This is an abbreviation used to reference the product that the chart is showing you. The ticker symbol on most stock platforms for a chart of Apple stock is AAPL; Google is GOOGL, Meta is FB. In the image above, we're looking at the NZDCAD (a spot Forex currency pair); that is the symbol at the top left.

However, the ticker symbol can be shown slightly differently depending on the platform. For example, you might see EURUSD or EUR.USD or EUR/USD or EURUSD.pro, which all refer to looking at a chart of the Euro versus the US dollar. You could see @ES or /ES or ES1!, which all refer to the continuous contract of the S&P Futures. You will get used to the particular symbols used on the platform or platforms you choose to use.

To change the ticker symbol to look at a different market, we can type in the symbol (if we know it) or choose from a dropdown menu and search the market we want to look at. To make this a quicker process in the future, we can create a personalized watchlist in order to have a preset list of symbols that we want to look at, and simply choose from our watchlist each time we trade.

Timeframes

Next to the ticker symbol, we can see the timeframe we are using, which refers to the lifespan of each candle, or how much time each candle is worth. For example, if we're looking at a daily chart, then that means that each candle on that chart is worth one day's trading. Therefore, you may be able to view months' worth of trading on one chart, with multiple daily candles filling your chart. If we are looking at a five-minute chart, then that means that each candle is worth five minutes of trading. So, you might see hours to days' worth of trading on your chart at one time, with multiple five-minute candles filling the chart.

Understanding the use of timeframes is important, as observing different timeframes may reveal clues that help define which type of trades to execute, if any. Think about what a doctor might do if a patient comes in with an injured knee – most likely, take a collection of X-rays, all from different angles, to get a better picture of what's going on and make it easier to diagnose a break or a sprain. If they just took one X-ray from one angle, they may end up coming to the wrong conclusion.

This is the same with our trades: if you only look at one timeframe chart, you will only have a partial view of the markets and, therefore, your view may not represent what is truly happening.

For example, let's say you see a move on an eight-minute timeframe chart, where each candle is worth eight minutes of price movement. You see what looks like a huge move to the upside, with a big blue or green candle. But if you were to switch to the 60-minute chart, where each candle is worth an hour of price movement, then the move may not look so significant.

If you look at one chart only, it may give the impression that the market is going to the moon, but maybe the reality is it's actually in a relatively boring mood compared to other timeframes.

Sometimes, we can see a trend, or climate, on a particular timeframe, but if we changed timeframes on the same product, we would see an opposite trend. For example, an uptrend on a 60-minute chart may be a small reversal on a longer-term downtrend on a daily chart, so for us to be more precise and accurate with our trades, we will use multiple timeframes each time we trade to guide our decisions.

We can switch timeframes in our platforms, usually by typing in the timeframe we want or choosing from a drop-down menu. The majority of platforms will allow you to view your charts using a standard set of timeframes, such as 15-minute, 60-minute, 240-minute (or four-hour), daily, etc. These are standard and very commonly used.

There are some platforms that also allow you to view custom timeframe charts that are outside the usual set of timeframes. For example, an eight-minute chart, or a 21-minute chart, or a 55-minute chart. These are all uncommon timeframes to view. TradingView allow you to see both standard and custom timeframes (TradingView access to custom timeframes comes with the Pro Plan and above).

On a lot of platforms, there will also be a watermark on the chart that shows what market you are looking at, as well as the timeframe you are looking at.

CANDLE FORMATION

When we say "candle," we mean the colored bar on the chart that shows us price movement. Most charts are viewed using candlesticks. As we mentioned before, one candle can be worth whatever period of time we want depending on the timeframe that we choose to view. If we choose a weekly timeframe, then each candle shows us price movement for one week. If we choose a two-minute timeframe, then each candle shows us price movement for one, two-minute period. Each candle can be one of two colors and has four price points:

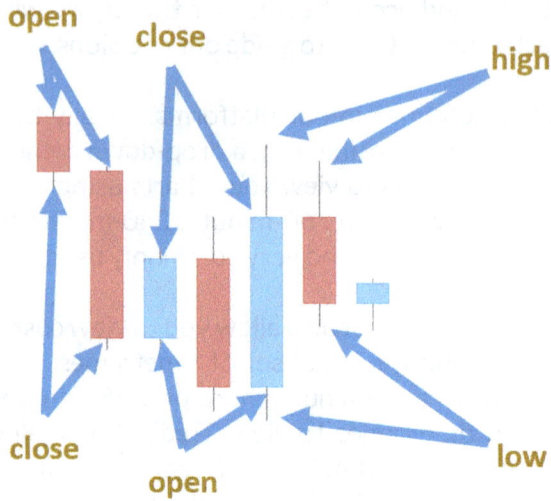

"Up" candles are usually depicted in blue or green and show us that price closed higher than it opened within that given time period. If we look at a 30-minute chart and a candle is green or blue, it means that, by the end of that 30-minute period, price was higher than at the beginning of that 30-minute period.

"Down" candles are usually depicted in red and follow the opposite pattern. If we look at a 30-minute chart and a candle is red, it means that, by the end of the 30-minute period, price was lower than what it was at the beginning of the same time period.

High = the very top of the candle. This tells us the highest price that the market reached within the given timeframe. If the picture above was a 21-minute chart, then the high would be the highest price reached within that 21-minute period.

Low = the very bottom of the candle. This tells us the lowest price that the market reached within the given timeframe.

Highs and lows are the same reference value whatever the color (or direction) of the candle.

The little vertical lines that we see above and below the main body of the candles in the image shown are what we call "wicks." They show us the full range of price movement within the time period that the candle refers to. The "body" of the candle (the thicker colored section) shows us the difference between open and closing prices of the candle.

Open = where price was at the start (or "open") of the given period of time.

In the case of "up" candles, which are normally depicted as blue or green, the open is at the bottom of the body of the candle.

In the case of "down" candles, which are normally depicted as red, the open is at the top of the body of the candle.

Close = where price was at the end (or "close") of the given period of time.

In the case of "up" candles, the close is at the top of the body of the candle.

In the case of "down" candles, the close is at the bottom of the body of the candle.

The color of the candles can be changed and are not always shown to be green/blue and red. In fact, you could change the color of all of your candles to gray and the high, low, open and close information would be the same, but it would be harder for us to tell the difference by looking at an individual candle.

TERMINOLOGY CORNER

It's helpful to understand some terminology that we will be using throughout the book, so you can come back for easy reference as you move through the methodology.

Liquidity

Refers to the likelihood of finding a counterparty to fill our orders. In other words, the likelihood of finding buyers when you want to sell or the likelihood of finding sellers when you want to buy. The higher the liquidity, the more likely we are to enter and exit our trades at the exact price we wanted to.

As traders, we love liquidity, as it's easier to get in and out of the markets we're trading, given the number of participants in them. Liquidity is not volume, although they are heavily linked.

Volume

Refers to the number of units traded in a market. Of course, if a market is very liquid and has a lot of market participants, then it makes sense that they will probably trade a lot and, therefore, you will have a lot of trades (or units traded). Usually, high liquidity produces high volume and low liquidity produces low volume.

However, this is not always the case. Let's say the S&P is very liquid, but the day before Thanksgiving there is little volume (in terms of the number of trades that are executed). It's not that the market is not liquid, it just means that maybe that day there were fewer trading hours and, the end result was, fewer trades were executed.

Slippage

Refers to being filled at a worse price than expected. Slippage is something that happens when a market is not liquid, so we are less likely to get a fill for our buy or sell order at the exact price that we want, because there are fewer market participants willing to take the other side of that trade.

Being filled at a worse price than expected adds risk. For example, if you're looking at a chart of an illiquid market, say you place a buy order at 3.21 and price moves quickly, and you see you got filled at 3.25, so you bought at a lot more expensive price than you wanted to. That is because, when you buy, someone needs to sell to you and, if there were not that many sellers, then they can take advantage and raise their ask to a higher price, so you got filled higher than expected.

The way to avoid slippage is to trade liquid markets. Of course, a good broker will also minimize slippage, but even if you used the best broker in the world to trade an illiquid market, you could still be hurt by slippage.

FOREX WATCHLIST

We mentioned our watchlists before, referring to a list of markets that we choose to trade and having them preset in our platform to more easily find their ticker symbols.

Within Forex, we trade one currency against another and they come in pairs. There are two main lists that are commonly used:

MAJORS

These are the most liquid currency pairs in the world and they are all connected to the US dollar. Eighty percent of transactions worldwide are done using the US dollar, so it is by far the most liquid currency in the world, therefore the majors are extremely liquid currency pairs.

FX (Majors)	Add Symbol	≡
Symbol	Last	Chng (%)
AUDUSD	0.6867^{7}	+0.00071 (+0.10%)
EURUSD	1.1020^{4}	−0.00227 (−0.21%)
GBPUSD	1.2364^{2}	+0.00118 (+0.10%)
NZDUSD	0.6419^{9}	−0.00032 (−0.05%)
USDCAD	1.3150^{4}	−0.00016 (−0.01%)
USDCHF	0.9931^{8}	+0.00141 (+0.14%)
USDJPY	107.70^{6}	+0.170 (+0.16%)

MINORS (OR CROSS PAIRS)

This list may include the USD (for example, right at the bottom of the list in the following image), but only for pairs that have lower liquidity. In the case of the following image, the bottom pair refers to the US dollar versus the Singapore dollar. Although this pair is liquid enough to be traded, it's not the best in the world, so that's why it's not on the Majors list.

The majority of the pairs under this list are what are known as "cross pairs." This means there is no US dollar involved in the pair, like in the majority of examples in the following list; we have the Australian dollar versus the Canadian dollar, the Australian dollar versus the Swiss franc, the Australian dollar versus the Japanese yen, the Australian dollar versus the New Zealand dollar, and so on.

These currency pairs do not include the US dollar but are still very liquid. Combined across the two lists, we have 30 currency pairs that are liquid enough to trade. You can use these as your watchlist for Forex initially, or subtract some if you want to be more specific on the markets you trade.

Our watchlists can be dynamic. However, it's not like stocks, where you have 9,000 stocks in the US market and you may want to screen for good stocks every day and refresh your list once a day or once a week. In trading currencies, you are likely to use the lists above for a long time without needing to change them too much, if you don't want to.

FX (Minors)	Add Symbol	☰
Symbol	Last	Chng (%)
AUDCAD	0.9031^2	+0.00087 (+0.10%)
AUDCHF	0.6821^5	+0.00167 (+0.25%)
AUDJPY	73.97^0	+0.193 (+0.26%)
AUDNZD	1.0697^0	+0.00195 (+0.18%)
CADCHF	0.7552^9	+0.00119 (+0.16%)
CADJPY	81.90^4	+0.145 (+0.18%)
CHFJPY	108.43^9	+0.043 (+0.04%)
EURAUD	1.6046^3	−0.00489 (−0.30%)
EURCAD	1.4491^3	−0.00314 (−0.22%)
EURCHF	1.0945^4	−0.00084 (−0.08%)
EURGBP	0.8913^7	−0.00212 (−0.24%)
EURJPY	118.69^5	−0.056 (−0.05%)
EURNZD	1.7164^0	−0.00230 (−0.13%)
GBPAUD	1.8001^0	−0.00020 (−0.01%)
GBPCAD	1.6256^6	+0.00129 (+0.08%)
GBPCHF	1.2278^8	+0.00305 (+0.25%)
GBPJPY	133.15^2	+0.324 (+0.24%)
GBPNZD	1.9254^9	+0.00339 (+0.18%)
NZDCAD	0.8442^3	−0.00032 (−0.04%)
NZDCHF	0.6376^5	+0.00070 (+0.11%)
NZDJPY	69.14^7	+0.087 (+0.13%)
USDSGD	1.3790^6	−0.00074 (−0.05%)

TRADING TECHNOLOGY

Once the market data flows into a trading platform, we can either interpret that information by doing manual tasks or use the power of technology to automate this process. Since the markets became electronically traded decades ago and major market players are using technology for their trading, limiting analysis to manual methods, or doing things by hand, carries great disadvantages.

Apart from adding probabilities or saving time, these technological tools are key to making sure that traders always run mechanical processes when trading. Being mechanical is absolutely key, as mechanical equals consistent action – and consistent action is the only recipe to get consistent results.

If your action was random and you had consistent results, this is simply because you got lucky, as it would be against probabilities.

Drawing lines by hand, doing calculations by hand, identifying opportunities with your eye, are all processes that are likely to be at risk of human error. It would be understandable and expected for a trader to make a mistake whilst doing these exercises.

It's also very expectable that the trader could be biased and subjective. They may draw the line in a place one day and draw it somewhere else another day based on how they feel or think or based on other factors that have affected their thought process. A lot of traders say they have a "hunch" about a particular stock, or that a certain trade "looks good" or "feels right," as if there is an intuition about the markets that they can tune into. The simple, and perhaps harsh, fact of the matter is that the market does not care how we feel, think or intuit.

Many times, we can be in trades that we are sure will work out, then something unexpected happens in the markets and it goes against us. Or we rule out an opportunity because it "looks bad," or someone told us something we didn't like about the market, and then we see that it would have worked out in our favor if we'd taken it.

One of the issues with using gut feeling, intuition, manual processes and strategies, based only on our minds and eyes, is that the way we approach the markets can change based on entirely subjective factors: hunger, tiredness, stress, emotions, etc. This leads to inconsistent action, which, as we know, leads to inconsistent results.

As traders, we need to think like businesspeople, risk managers and data analysts. We need to apply objective rules and automated processes so that we can be consistent in our approach, increasing the probability that our results are consistent, and removing human error as much as possible.

Trading technology takes a lot of those potential issues out of the equation and does a lot of the work for us, which saves us time and performs the work in a mechanical and objective way. In trading technology apps, rules must be programmed based on objective data. A machine will not be inhibited by anything psychological or personal and cannot be biased; the markets are either providing the data that leads to an opportunity, or they are not.

Classical Indicators

There are different types of trading technology tools depending on the trading platforms being used. Technical indicators, studies or trading apps are often words that mean the same thing. These tools process market data and automatically return results that can be used to define specific trade setups and execute trades accordingly.

Most platforms are programmable, meaning you can program your strategy yourself into the platform. TradingView is programmable and allow users to input their own rules and strategies using the market data gathered from these platforms. Although some people may know how to program, or have great technology expertise, most people who trade, do not have technical expertise to that level, so they will use apps that already exist to assist them with their trading decisions. Some apps or indicators that are commonly used are:

- Moving Averages
- Ichimoku Cloud
- Bollinger Bands®
- Average True Range (ATR)
- Directional Movement Index (DMI)
- Moving Average Convergence Divergence (MACD)
- Relative Strength Index (RSI)
- Fibonacci Retracement Tools

These are just a few of the indicators that are available to use on most trading platforms and that traders use every day to help them analyze the markets and make decisions about their trades. They can be good tools that are useful in certain contexts, depending on what you are trying to do with them.

However, the problem with these types of tools is that most answer the same question, so they all produce confirmation of the same thing. However, the traders who use them, often fail to look at the market with as many angles as are needed, and therefore the trades may not be precise enough and therefore not successful enough.

Most classical indicators have a lagging effect since they use large amounts of data from the past in their computations. This often causes people to get into a trade once a move has already happened, so they enter late to the party. The move could keep going and they make profits, but since they've entered after it's already started, they have less probability of it continuing, and more probability that they were too late, with the move ending soon after they enter the trade.

The tools we use as traders should give us an edge in the markets. The apps and technologies above are available for free on most platforms and are extremely accessible to the general public. Some apps are more specialized and may not be available on all platforms; others may require a subscription.

SPECIALIZED APPS

No matter what apps or technology you use to trade, every trading methodology should answer these questions:

1. Should I be a buyer or a seller? Or should I simply avoid trading?
2. If I trade, what is potentially an ideal buying price and what is potentially an ideal selling price?

These questions could be answered using the tools above, or other technology, but this is something we have to focus on. We do not want to waste our time buying or selling when the best thing to do is sit on our hands and keep out of the markets.

In our normal lives we have been taught that we exchange time for money so the more time I put in, the more money I make. The opposite is true in the markets: We do not want to spend time placing trades if they do not carry enough probability as that will lead to more losses and subsequent frustration. We do not want to trade to fill time. We want to trade only because we have an objective reason to get into a trade, based on data showing that it carries enough probabilities to be worth our risk and time.

Two of the specialized apps that we will show are AutoClimate™ and AutoUFOs®:

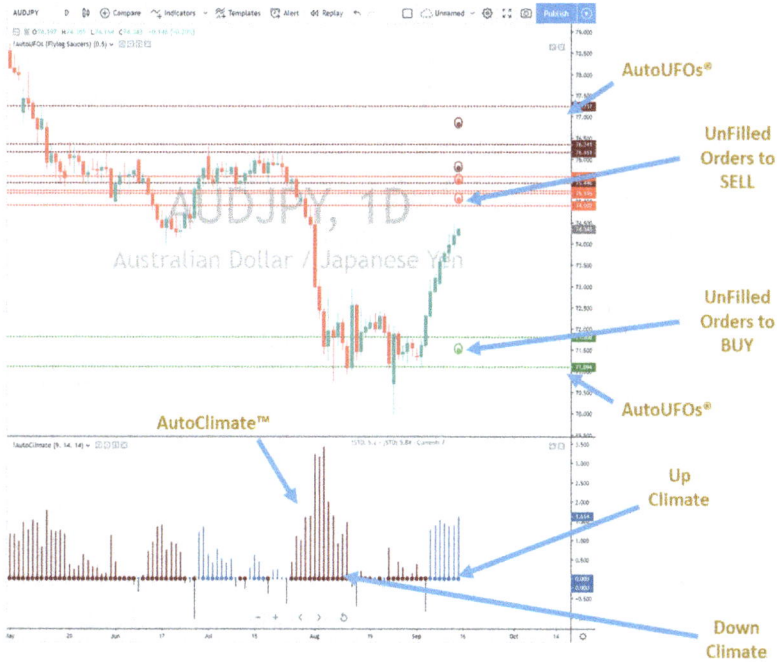

We use these apps to help answer the two questions that we have as traders.

AutoClimate™ is an app that analyzes market data and tells us the direction (or trend) of the market. It helps us to answer whether or not we should be a buyer or a seller. If the dot is thick and red, we should be a seller; if the dot is thick and blue, we should be a buyer. If the dot is thin (of either color), then we do nothing, which, as we already know, is a perfectly valid trading stance.

AutoUFOs® help us find areas for entry into trades, essentially answering the question of where the best buying or selling prices are. UFO stands for "UnFilled Orders." When big-market players buy or sell in the market, they often don't buy everything they want all at once, or sell everything they want all at once. They simply have too many orders.

This means that often there are stacks of buy or sell orders left behind in the markets waiting to be filled.

In other words, if a bank or an investment fund bought a lot of a particular product before, they probably didn't buy everything they wanted in one go, so they will want to buy there again. If they sold a lot of a particular product, they probably didn't sell everything they wanted in one go, so they will want to sell there again.

For example, a huge investment fund may have wanted to buy 500,000 shares of Apple in a particular price range. Maybe only 200,000 sellers were available at that time, so the investment fund still has 300,000 buy orders left in the market that are UnFilled. They are unlikely to cancel their orders, as they often would have a reason for the initial order size; if price returns to the same price range, there are still 300,000 orders to buy waiting, which are likely to turn price back up again.

These buy and sell orders that are left are picked up by the AutoUFOs® app, which shows the areas of price on a chart that are more likely to have big stacks of orders. If price returns to these areas, it is likely to turn back again. This works in our favor; if we execute at these UFOs, we are among the first in line to catch the move, as we'd catch it from the beginning.

The AutoUFOs® app shows UnFilled buy orders in green and UnFilled sell orders in red. This helps us to identify areas to enter, so that we buy when big market players buy and we sell when they sell, giving us an edge in the markets and a higher probability of success. Combined with AutoClimate™, we add even more odds in our favor.

To put it simply, AutoClimate™ helps us with question No. 1: Should we be a buyer or seller, or not trade? AutoUFOs® help us with question No. 2: What is the ideal buying price and the ideal selling price?

We will expand on these apps as we go through more content in the book.

ENTRIES AND EXITS

ENTRIES

Entries refer to the action of initiating a trade or adding more to an existing position (increasing the position size). There are two possible types of entries:

- Long Entry (entering to make money as price goes up)
- Short Entry (entering to make money as price goes down)

LONG ENTRY

Long entries are executed when a trader is attempting to make profit from a price move to the upside. In most markets, this is done simply by clicking the "buy" button, meaning that the trade is not over until clicking the "sell" button. When traders say things like "I'm long" or "I have a long position" or "I took a long entry", this is what they mean: they entered, in order to make profit on an upwards move in price.

If we buy to enter the market, there are two things that could happen: Price could go up and we make a profit by selling at a higher price, or price could go down and we would take a loss by selling at a lower price (at our stop-loss).

Using AutoUFOs®, we "go long" using the green UFOs that appear on our charts, as this is where we have probability that price could turn and go back up, and we want to make profit as price goes up. This is a snap-shot of going long using AutoUFOs® on the TradingView platform:

SHORT ENTRY

Short entries are the opposite to long entries: they are executed when a trader attempts to make a profit from a price move to the downside. In most markets, this is done by clicking the "sell" button, which means we get out of the trade for either a profit or loss by clicking the "buy" button. This is referred to as "shorting," "going short," "entering short" and variations of these phrases.

If we sell to enter a market, two things can happen: Price moves down and we collect profit by buying at a lower price, or price goes up and we take a loss by buying at a higher price (once again, at our stop-loss)

Going Short can confuse people. Everybody understands buying then selling; we are used to it in life and, even if we've never traded before, the concept makes sense to us. In reality, shorting is just as simple:

instead of buying then selling, we sell then buy. However, if this is the first time you've been exposed to the idea of shorting, it can be hard to understand how that is done. The most common question is: "How can I sell something I don't already own?"

The short answer is: Borrow it first.

If you borrow something, you need to return it. It is not yours, and you do not own it. Consequently, if you sell it and then buy it back, you must return it. If you were to go short on a stock and the market goes down, and then you buy at a lower price, you keep the difference and give back the stock.

Think of a physical product, let's say a TV. You borrow your friend's spare TV and sell it to someone for $500. You then go to a store you know has a sale and buy the exact same TV for $400. You give your friend back the exact same TV, but you keep a $100 profit. This profit would be the same if you bought the TV first for $400 then sold it for $500; you just reversed the order of transactions.

When you do this in the financial markets, you are borrowing the stock, contract, commodity, etc., from your broker. You then sell it and, if price moves down, you buy it back and give the broker back the stock, contract or commodity, keeping the difference as profit. If price moves up and you buy back at a higher price, then you buy back the product, lose the difference and return the product to your broker.

Using the TV analogy: You borrow your friend's spare TV and sell it for $500, but go to the store and realize it's not on sale and the retail price is $600. You owe your friend the TV, so you buy it back for $600 and return the TV. You lose $100 in this scenario. This loss is exactly the same as if you'd bought the TV first for $600 then sold it for $500.

In the financial markets, all the borrowing is done electronically, automatically and at the speed of light; we don't need to worry about how this happens. We just click "sell" and we will have automatically borrowed the product and sold it.

Our brokers are happy to lend us financial products (stocks, futures contracts, currencies, etc.) to sell to others; to them, whether you buy it back for a profit or loss, they still have the exact product. Their business is not in the value of the products they hold, but in the commissions they charge per transaction.

If we, as their customers, are able to both buy and sell to get into a position, we pay them twice the amount of commission so they're very happy to lend us products they don't care about the value of, and to collect extra commissions. Like your friend with the TV, they don't care about the value of the TV, whether you made or lost money – they still get back the exact same TV.

The risk of going long is exactly the same as going short. If you buy something, it can go down and you lose money. If you sell something, it can go up and you lose money. If you buy first at $10 and then sell at $12, you make the same as if you sell first at $12 and buy back at $10. Either way it is the same; shorting is nothing to fear or avoid.

Using AutoUFOs®, we go short using the red UFOs that appear on our charts; this is where we have probability that price could turn and go back down, and we want to make profit as price goes down. This is a snapshot of going short using AutoUFOs® on the TradingView platform:

Exits

Exits refers to the action of closing our position (fully or partially). There are two types of possible exits:

- Exit at a loss
- Exit for a profit

This can be done by clicking the "sell" button if you're in a long position or the "buy" button if you're in a short position. This will close the position, so you are no longer in the trade and you have either profited or lost.

LOSING EXITS

This is where you close a losing position as a consequence of a market not behaving as expected. If you expect the market to go up and you're long, and instead the market goes down, you execute a sell order and you exit the trade for a loss. If you expect the market to go down and you're short, and instead the market goes up, then you execute a buy order and you exit the trade for a loss.

We covered this already in the book, but we will cover it again and again: We always, always, always use stops!

Stop-loss orders automate the action of exiting a trade for a loss. This helps us to execute these orders whilst avoiding procrastination and the impact of human emotions. We place a stop-loss at a predefined price based on data, which is a price where we are proved wrong for the smallest risk. Some traders like to use manual exits, known as "mental" stop-loss orders. This could be valid in some cases, but it certainly exposes traders to the dangers of being emotional beings. Even something as simple as forgetting, could result in a huge loss that could be easily rectified with an automatic order.

If we are going long and therefore buying to enter a position, our stop-loss (in this case a sell stop) will be below our entry. We want to have a predefined price so that if we're wrong (and we are going to be wrong sometimes), we are not risking too much money and we can afford to trade another day.

In the example below, we would of course much rather be out of the trade where our sell stop was, rather than still be holding onto it at the bottom. We want to enter where there are UnFilled Orders, but sometimes those orders can be canceled and, if that's the case, then we don't want to still be in the trade if price moves against us.

If we are going short and therefore selling to enter a position, then our stop-loss must be above our entry (this will be a buy stop). If we want to sell, expecting price to go down, but instead it goes up, we get out of the trade at a predefined loss.

In the example below, we would be much happier to be out of the trade where our buy stop is, losing much less than if we were still short and price had gone really far against us.

PROFITABLE EXITS

This is a trading action where the trader closes a winning position based on trading rules. This may imply scaling out of a position (taking out chunks of profit as the market moves in our favor) or fully closing a position.

Scaling out could be done for risk management purposes (we call this a Safety Target) to quickly remove risk attached to a trade if price does start to move in your favor. This could allow other trades to be taken in parallel without increasing portfolio risk.

This also makes it psychologically easier if you're attempting to capture large moves in the markets. For instance, you may have a risk-to-reward ratio of 1:10, so your target is 10:1 away from your entry. Waiting for a price to reach all the way to 10:1 and watching it stall – and maybe retrace a bit on its way – can be hard, from a mental point of view but taking chunks of profit on the way to the target means you are much more likely to let it run, as you are collecting something on your way there.

We may have a Safety Target (used for removing risk quickly, psychological calm, or locking in profits) and also a Final Target (where we want to get out fully from our position).

When using AutoUFOs®, we use the "rival UFO" as our Final Target location. If we go long, we use a green UFO for our entry, our sell stop goes below the green UFO, and our final target will be at the red UFO, such as in the image below:

If we go short, we use a red UFO for our entry, our buy stop goes above the UFO and our final target will be at the green UFO, such as in the following image:

We need to get used to planning our losses as much as planning our profits. It's better to have a plan in case we're wrong so that it doesn't hurt us so much. For every trade, we will have an Entry, a Stop and a Target predefined.

MARKET CLIMATE

The first question we need to answer as traders is: Should I be a buyer, seller, or not trade at all? Essentially, we want to know if we have enough probabilities to take a trade and, if so, in which direction. If the answer to Question 1 is not to trade at all on the market we're looking at, then we move on and look at something else. If the next thing we look at also answers Question 1 with "don't trade," then we move on to something else, and so on. Sometimes we will see that we simply don't have an opportunity to trade in the markets we look at. It can be hard to choose not to trade; we can feel like we're not being productive, as we're so used to exchanging time for money. There are many traders who have incredible knowledge when it comes to the markets or methodologies, but they don't have rules to <u>not</u> trade, which can be problematic and lead to unnecessary losses.

It is much more efficient to not trade when we don't have probability and overall have fewer losses. Let's say you trade ten times and seven times you lose and three times you win. You may still make money if you have a good reward-to-risk ratio, but what if you simply didn't take three of those losers because you chose not to enter the markets when you had less probability? Then you would have, overall, had seven trades: three winners and four losers. With the same reward-to-risk ratio, you would have, overall, made more money and have traded less.

This could be the difference between struggling for profits and making money consistently, while also saving your time. Think of it as increasing your hourly wage!

We need to have a rule that tells us when we can trade and when we should do nothing. If we do trade, we need to know in which direction, long or short?

A lot of traders will want to follow the trend to help them know whether to go long or short. Even if you've never traded before, you've probably heard the phrase "the trend is your friend". This is a classic statement in most trading books and methodologies.

Let's say that to identify the trend, you use an indicator –for example, Ichimoku Cloud – which will help you answer the question of whether you go long or short. Now you need to answer Question 2, which is: Where is the best price to buy or sell? Now you use another indicator, such as Bollinger Bands®, or you draw support and resistance lines and enter at a breakout, or you look at chart patterns and use them to identify your entry price.

The problem with using indicators like this, however, is that they will never tell you not to trade. Your trend-identifying indicator will simply say "up" or "down," "buy" or "sell," but never "don't trade", so you go through a process to identify an entry when maybe you shouldn't have been trading at all. Moreover, when you get to deciding your entry price, you are using indicators that follow price, so you're depending on price movement to find your entry, which means you're more likely to have to act manually. That's not necessarily wrong, but acting manually may invoke emotional behavior, like chasing the market, which has you buying at higher prices and selling at lower prices, which ultimately reduces your probability and reward capability.

What we propose is that you develop a methodology where everything is peaceful, where you get clear answers to what you should be doing and where your execution can be consistent and mechanical.

Returning to how we answer Question 1, it is a good thing to identify trend, but we also need to know when not to trade. The use of AutoClimate™ allows us to have the answer to this question in its entirety.

Market Climate can be seen as the current Market Environment, or what direction the market is moving in. When we go on holiday, we might want to look at what the climate will be so that we can pack accordingly. Let's say we're going to Spain in September; we look it up and we see that it's not as sunny as it is in August, but it's still quite hot so we pack for summer. There might be a higher probability of rain, so we might pack an umbrella. Although right now it might be August, and the weather is hot and sunny with a low probability of rain, we know that this could change. Climate goes way beyond the weather that is happening now; it goes into understanding what is likely to happen next. We don't have a guarantee that the climate will make the weather behave exactly as we predict, but we have higher probabilities to make a good plan if we understand what the climate is like in Spain in September.

For our trading, it is the same: we want to use probabilities to help us understand the climate so we can create a good plan around our execution. A key concept in our trading is that we need to embrace lasting trends. Lasting trends don't mean that your trades need to last five weeks or five months; it means that whatever timeframe you trade in, you can stay in a trend as long as possible.

For example, if you trade using the five-minute timeframe, you may want to continue in the same direction for 10 to 20 candles, which would happen over 50 minutes to an hour and 40 minutes. If you were to trade a bigger time-frame, say the weekly timeframe, and you were to follow a trend for 20 candles, then you'd be in the trade for around five months. We want our trends to last, which means that price will be traveling towards our targets, leading to making bigger profits and smaller losses.

What we want to avoid is entering a climate that is about to change, like if it's sunny for a couple of days and then rains. You may want to enjoy the sun for a couple of days but if the market only moves in your favor for a couple of candles, you will end up with profits of a smaller size and, most likely losses that are more than, or equal to, the size of the profits.

This isn't necessarily wrong; as long as you win more often, you can still make money. But remember that we are looking for balance. We want to win relatively often and have our profits be bigger than our losses.

Some market characteristics tend to last. This offers higher-probability trades and longer-lasting trades. Adding odds to our trades reduces the number of times when a market shows unexpected behavior. Longer-lasting trades expose trades to bigger market movements, which helps us maximize the size of our profits. This creates more balance, which is what we're looking for as traders.

Market Characteristics

Market Trends

Classically defined by the overall direction that the market is moving, which could be up, down or perhaps sideways (where price is moving horizontally within a range). As we already discussed, the classical way to identify this is an incomplete analysis and understanding of the market environment, but it is something useful to understand. If a market is moving in a certain direction, meaning the overall direction is either up or down, then the market is only moving in that direction because there are more buyers on a consistent basis so price keeps moving up, or there are more sellers on a consistent basis, so price keeps moving down.

Market trends are just like other trends in life, like fashion trends. Something becomes popular because other people are doing it. Trends last for a while because more people get involved, and then they change and a new trend starts. For example, if a particular color is popular to wear, it may be popular for a while, and then a new color becomes popular. This is the same in the markets: Trends last because a lot of people are following the same idea and doing the same thing. It has more probability to work for us, as long as we don't get in towards the end of the trend.

Market Sustainability

Refers to the amount of distance and time price spent travelling in a specific direction and, therefore, the likelihood of this condition to remain or change. Let's say the average fashion trend, in terms of what color to wear, lasts for around nine months and, currently, purple is the "in" color – it's very trendy and everyone is wearing it. You look at how long purple has been the trend and you see that it's been around nine months already, so although the trend may still be purple for now, it is much more likely to change sometime soon.

Of course, it could last a little longer and go on for ten months, maybe twelve months but, the longer it goes on, the less likely it is to carry on being the trend. The same is true in the markets; trends are created by human behavior and trading software is programmed by people so even algorithms are based on human behavior.

If we have a trend in a particular market that usually lasts for 55 candles, and it's currently candle number 75, we know we have less probability that this will continue in the same direction. Entering a trade too late in the trend or, even worse, beyond the usual sustainability of a trend – would be too hopeful, as it would go against probabilities. We use the statistics of sustainability to help us be more objective and not enter trades based on opinions. The markets are bigger than us, so we need to be adaptable and flexible and not be opinionated.

A very old saying in the world of trading is "a market can remain irrational for longer than you could remain solvent". The history of trading is full of people that had very strong opinions about a market only to enter trades and get badly hurt.

Our job is to put our opinions on the side when it comes to our trading. We rely on objective, measurable, quantifiable data that allows us to plan with probabilities on our side, even though sometimes market behavior will move away from what probabilities suggest. Probabilities imply that a collection of things could happen, although there could be some anomalies, and that's okay. We still want to make sure we are focused on what is more likely to happen and discard what is less likely to happen.

Market Volatility

This refers to the speed of price movement or how far price moves within given periods of time. Let's say you look at a market and it's moving in an overall upwards direction and sustainability is also on your side because the move has only just started. You may look at this opportunity and decide the odds are good enough for you to enter a trade. However, if the speed of movement on that market is very low, you may be in that trade waiting to hit your target for a long time. This would increase the chances that sustainability dies out and the market environment changes, as well as tying up your capital for a long time, which may reduce your ability to take other opportunities. Even though the trend is in your favor, and it looks to be sustainable, you may discard these types of trades for being inefficient.

If the market was to be much more volatile, and you are equipped with the right tools, you have room to make money at a higher pace. As an experienced trader, you will love fast market movements. We like to be wrong quickly, or right quickly. However, if you are newer to trading, higher volatility can trigger and challenge your emotions more as you will have to make decisions faster. You may be stopped out and then given an opportunity to re-enter the same market, hesitate on it because you've just taken a loss, and then miss the opportunity. From this, it's common to develop unconscious anger and, the next thing you know, you are trading in "revenge mode" and you want back the money you lost.

Our approach is survival to mastery so, when you start, you would probably expose yourself to markets that move at a more relaxed pace until you develop the skill to a point where you are very comfortable executing your plan.

More importantly, after developing skill, you will have something much stronger, which is confidence in your plan and in yourself to operate your plan and see results. This can only happen through practice.

As we develop, we become more confident that our stop-loss will take care of the bad side of volatility. If we are wrong, we will be wrong either way, whether price moves fast or slow. Our stop will get us out at our pre-determined price and we'd rather that happen quickly so that we can move on to the next trade. Very, very rarely would our stop be compromised in a high-volatility market.

In 2012, the Swiss National Bank decided to peg the Swiss Franc to the Euro. All the currency pairs with the Swiss Franc moved at a crazy and unprecedented pace, about ten times more than was normal at the time. This resulted in slippage, which is something we covered earlier, where we would get stopped out at a worse price than expected and so took a greater loss than expected.

It can also happen the other way, where volatility increases slippage and we get filled at a better price for our target and end up profiting more than expected. In most cases, though, slippage does not occur very often and our stops will protect us at a predefined price.

AUTOCLIMATE™

AutoClimate™ is a trading app that answers Question No. 1: Should I be a buyer or a seller? Or should I simply avoid trading and not trade at all?

AutoClimate™ identifies market trend as either defined (confirmed) or undefined (unconfirmed). When the market climate is defined, a trader would want to be a buyer or a seller. When the climate is undefined – the direction is clear, but you don't have statistical information that tells you more about sustainability, or you have sustainability information but the overall direction is unclear – then a trader should avoid trading.

The AutoClimate™ indicator shows at the bottom of the chart, as shown below:

(TradingView):

(MT5):

AutoClimate™ is represented by dots (for now, ignore the lines that protrude from the dots). The dots are displayed in one of two colors: red or blue. We also call these colors ruby or sapphire, but we are referring to the same thing. The red (ruby) color dictates a downwards climate or downtrend. The blue (sapphire) color dictates an upwards climate or uptrend. On the left side of the chart above, we can see that the overall direction of the market is up, and the AutoClimate™ is showing us blue dots, telling us the market is in an upward climate.

There is a moment in time when the dots change color and begin to show as red, telling us that the climate has changed, which we can then see from what happens to price as it moves to the right. The use of technology helps us to identify this objectively and not confuse our human eye as to the direction of the market.

When the climate is not clearly confirmed, then the app will show the dot as a thin dot instead of a thick dot. The colors remain but the thickness is what tells us about the confirmed status of the climate. If the dot is thick, then it is time to trade in the direction that the color tells us (red = short, blue = long). If the dot is thin, then it is time to not trade. The color and thickness of the dots give us a very clear structure for our trading rules, essentially giving us three simple options at this stage:

THICK BLUE DOT = look for long opportunities

THICK RED DOT = look for short opportunities

THIN DOT OF EITHER COLOR = do not trade

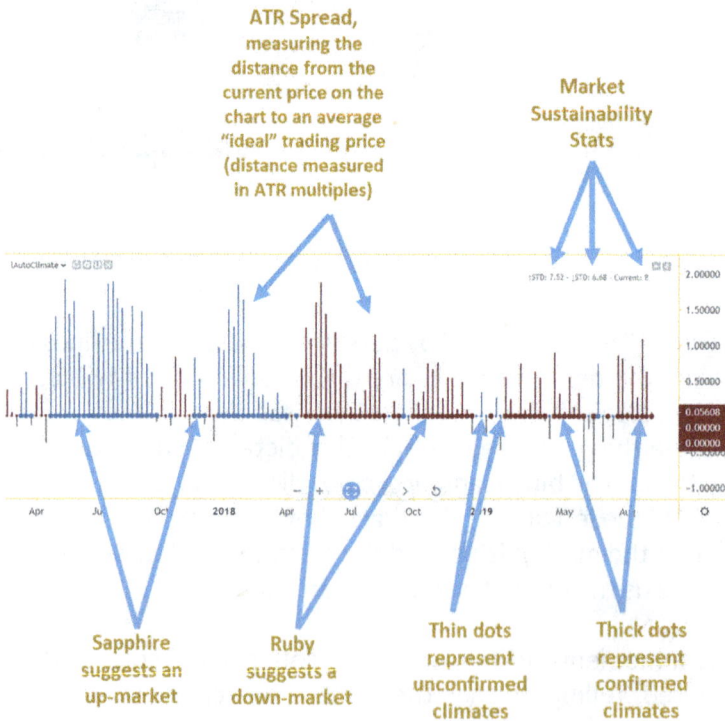

ATR Spread, measuring the distance from the current price on the chart to an average "ideal" trading price (distance measured in ATR multiples)

Market Sustainability Stats

Sapphire suggests an up-market

Ruby suggests a down-market

Thin dots represent unconfirmed climates

Thick dots represent confirmed climates

The question is not just about the overall direction of the market, but how likely that direction is to continue. This refers to sustainability. The app shows us sustainability data in the form of three figures, which are displayed above the dots.

The first figure references the stats for what tends to happen when the market, on that timeframe, goes up. In other words, when that market goes up, how long does it normally remain moving in that direction? If the figure is 6, normally that market goes up for 6 candles on that timeframe before changing direction.

The second figure references the same data but for down climates. When the market on that timeframe goes down, how long does it normally remain moving to the downside? If the number is 4, statistically speaking, that market goes down for 4 candles on that timeframe before changing direction.

The third figure shows us for how long the market has been moving in the given direction. Let's say the climate is up, so we see a blue dot on our AutoClimate™ app, and the first number shows us 5, and the third number shows us 2. This would mean we are currently 2 candles into a move to the upside, out of an average of 5 this market normally goes up for.

Everything with statistics is based on thousands of pieces of data and, of course, there are sometimes anomalies that happen outside of probabilities. Sometimes you will see that current sustainability figures are beyond statistical predictions. Let's say the climate is down (red dot on the app), the second sustainability figure is showing us 6, and the third number is showing 8. In this case, that particular market would normally go down for 6 candles before changing direction, but we are currently on the eighth candle moving to the downside. This tells us that the market has been moving for too long (statistically speaking) to the downside, and is now entering non-sustainable territory, where the climate is likely to change. It's been raining for too many days so tomorrow it's likely to be sunny.

Although a thick dot of either color gives you permission to trade, the sustainability stats may rule out an opportunity because the market has already been moving for too long in that direction and is likely to change. "The trend is your friend until the bend in the end", someone said.

Each of the dots that are shown on the AutoClimate™ display have a "tail", or a vertical line, coming out of the top of the dot. That line represents the distance from current price to what an ideal trading price would be. It is measured in multiples of the ATR, the Average True Range.

The ATR is a classical indicator available in all trading platforms that tells us how much the market moves averagely in a given timeframe. It is calculated by taking the high and low of the last 14 candles in a chart to give an average. It then tells us how much, as an average, each candle tends to move.

If we are looking at a daily chart and we open an ATR indicator, we see how much price moves averagely per day. This means that, if the ATR shows us 200 pips, that market averagely moves 200 pips in one day. If we look at a 55-minute chart and open an ATR indicator, we will find out how much price moves averagely per 55 minutes. If the ATR shows us 25 pips, that market averagely moves 25 pips in 55 minutes.

The vertical lines on our AutoClimate™ app tell us how far away (in multiples of ATR) the current price is from an ideal trading price. We will explain in a later chapter what an "ideal trading price" is. For now, let's accept that there is one, and that the ATR spread shown on AutoClimate™ is measuring how far current price is away from that ideal price.

What the app is telling us with those vertical lines is how overstretched a market is. If we see "2", for example, that price is two times the normal movement away from an ideal trading price. Let's say that the ATR on a daily chart was 150 pips, meaning price usually moves 150 pips a day, and the AutoClimate™ app is showing us an ATR spread of "2". This would mean that price is 300 pips away from an ideal trading price. That could mean that we would have to wait for a couple of days for price to be able to move back to where we ideally want to trade it.

A few more examples:

Let's say the ATR on a 21-minute chart is 15 pips, meaning price usually moves 15 pips in 21 minutes, and the AutoClimate™ app is showing us an ATR spread of "1". This would mean that price is 15 pips away from an ideal trading price and we may have to wait at least 21 minutes for price to be able to move back to where we'd ideally want to trade it.

If the ATR on a weekly chart is 500 pips, meaning price usually moves 500 pips in a week, and the AutoClimate™ app is showing us a spread of "0.5", that price is 250 pips from an ideal trading price, and we might wait half a week for price to retrace to an ideal trading price.

If price is very overstretched and far away from an ideal trading price, we may not want to go further on that market to look for trading opportunities to execute. This could mean we'll be waiting for a while to get into a higher probability trade (depending on the timeframe). If we're waiting a while, this could mean that conditions change by the time price gets back to the ideal trading price (like the climate has changed, or we are coming to the end of the climate's sustainability). By that point, we would rule out the trade based on climate direction, confirmation or sustainability.

We also wouldn't want to look further into a trade setup, only to get tempted to enter the market at the wrong price, when we know the ideal trading price is much further away. We would simply move on to look at markets that are much closer to an ideal trading price, providing the climate is confirmed and we have probability that the climate is likely to continue to propagate.

The advantage of using technology to calculate these figures for us is that it removes a lot of subjectivity and human error when it comes to not only identifying trend, but how long the trend may last. We can also often program the technology to alert us when the right conditions have been met (objectively) so we use our time efficiently when looking for trading opportunities.

We usually want to look for opportunities in markets that are 0.5 or less when it comes to the ATR spread. In other words, we want to be efficient with our time and look for opportunities that are more likely to happen sooner.

Using AutoClimate™

Combining the three pieces of information that we get from the AutoClimate™ app, we have a clear structure about whether to trade and in which direction, and whether now is a good time to place the trade. If we do enter a trade because all three elements line up well, we put odds in our favor to get into a higher probability trade. Let's go into a few scenarios:

We see a **thick blue** dot, meaning we have a confirmed upwards climate. The market usually goes up for 6 candles and we are on candle number 2 so we have sustainability on our side. The ATR spread is 0.2 so it is very close to an ideal trading price.

Conclusion = look for LONG opportunities

We see a **thick red** dot, meaning we have a confirmed downwards climate. The market usually goes down for 8 candles and we are on candle number 3, so we also have sustainability on our side. However, the ATR spread is 3, so we are extremely overstretched and far from an ideal trading price; we'd have to wait awhile to get into a trade, meaning conditions may change by the time price moves back.

Conclusion = move on and look at another market closer to an ideal trading price

We see a **thin blue** dot, meaning we have an unconfirmed upwards climate.

Conclusion = do not trade. There is no need to look into any other statistics if we do not first have a confirmed climate

We see a **thick red** dot, meaning we have a confirmed downwards climate. However, the sustainability stats show us that normally this market moves down for 5 candles, and we are currently on candle number 12 so the market is extremely overextended to the downside.

Conclusion = do not trade. It is unlikely that the climate will continue.

ORDER FLOW

Order flow refers to the continuous process by which buy and sell orders keep coming in and out of a specific market. As you read this, there are people pressing "buy" and there are people pressing "sell" and those buy and sell orders are being sent to exchanges or interbank systems. If there is a buyer of a specific asset and a seller, then they will find each other electronically via those exchanges and interbank systems.

This is what we mean when we say "filled order"; it refers to a buy and sell, and transaction of an equal size, actually happening, so, if someone wants to buy 100 shares of stock and presses buy, and someone out there is selling 100 shares of stock, then the buyer's order is filled and all 100 shares purchased.

Order flow is critical in trading and investing. Without orders coming in and out of a market, the market cannot move. We see this when a market is closed. The US stock market, for example, is open from 9:30 a.m. EST to 4 p.m. EST, meaning it is open for 6.5 hours; this means it's closed for 17.5 hours. During the time the market is closed, price cannot move as no orders can reach the market.

The amount of buy versus sell orders dictates the movement of the market. If there are more buy orders than sell orders, price must go up. If there are more sell orders than buy orders, price must go down. Think about it like anything else in life: if there is a lot of buying of a product, the price of the product can go up, but if there is a limited number of buyers and various sellers, the price has to go down. This is exactly how financial markets work too.

The beauty of order flow in the markets is that, unlike products in real life, we can see everything that has already happened in terms of orders having been executed. We can see what orders were filled on which days and whether there were more buyers or sellers. The chart certainly represents order flow, but order flow that is gone. The order flow that we want to use as traders is that which is still available.

Depending on finding a valid counterparty, some of the orders that come into the market will be executed (and become Filled Orders) and some may be cancelled after a while.

Orders that are still waiting to be either executed or canceled are known as Un-Filled Orders (UFOs). This is not to be confused with Unidentified Flying Objects (although the app we use that plots them on the chart for us does show them as flying saucers!).

What the app is helping to do is identify where there are buy orders waiting to be executed and where there are sell orders waiting to be executed. We see the Un-Filled Orders on the chart depicted as green (buy) UFOs or red (sell) UFOs. We will explain the use of this technology later in the book.

DIRECT VS INDIRECT FORCES

There are many forces that may impact a market, such as news, reports, fundamentals, technical factors, even tweets! However, when a market is closed, these factors cannot influence the direction of price, because price cannot move. Price can only move when the trading session is open because that is the only time when buy and sell orders can be executed. In other words, if there was a major news report that was capable of impacting the market, but it was reported over the weekend when the market is closed, then no orders can be filled and the market cannot move. Although the reason for the movement would still be there, it cannot actually have an impact unless the market is open for buy and sell orders to move through it. It is the process of Un-Filled Orders becoming Filled (buy and sell orders that are actually executed) that moves price.

A sensible conclusion is that the flow of orders entering a market is the one direct force responsible for the movement of price. All other reasons (such as news, etc.) would be seen as indirect forces, since their potential influence would only translate in price movement, if and when a significant number of orders changed status from Un-Filled to Filled.

An extreme example of this could be natural disasters. Of course, tsunamis, earthquakes and hurricanes are catastrophic events that could have had a huge impact on various markets. But what if one happens over a weekend? The market cannot react as no orders can enter the market, despite the obvious reality of a natural disaster. We also know that there are some news reports that are fake or, perhaps, government data that is corrected the next day. These things that happen are not accurate, but they still could convince buyers or sellers to enter the markets.

Price movement happens, not because the news is fake or real, big or small but, because of orders. Ultimately, it is all down to the direct force of buy orders and sell orders.

As traders, our job is to catch a move and ride a move in the markets, meaning we enter a market and follow it in a profitable direction. To do this, we certainly do need to rely on the direct force of order flow but, we would suggest that we also go beyond this and use a combination of direct and indirect forces to increase our odds.

CHARACTERISTICS OF INDIRECT FORCES

News, reports, fundamentals, technical factors, etc. are subject to interpretation; large market players may act on them by adding or removing orders from the market and we will never know which they choose to do, if anything at all.

Interpretation is, by definition, subjective. It often puts the smaller market players at risk of being on the wrong side of the market. Part of the reason for this may be that large market players often have access to this type of information ahead of smaller market players so they can act on it first. As interpretation is subjective, they may have a different interpretation than we will, and it will be their orders that are more likely to move the market. Subjectivity cannot be a consistent approach

75

to the market as price moves based on objective reasons: buy orders and sell orders.

Indirect forces are indeed powerful reasons for markets to move but it is often problematic to plan trades exclusively based on this type of information as the outcome would often lack consistency. If price always went up after a particular fundamental report was positive, then it would be common knowledge and everyone would be able to capitalize on it, but this is not the case.

Sometimes, the market does the opposite of what most people would expect from the news or another kind of indirect force. Here is an example:

Important EUR News released at 10:00 AM GMT:
- The expected figure was worse than the prior one
- The EUR was falling already prior to the Report
- The prior figure was better than the reported one
- The real figure was worse than the expectation

Here we see that the EURUSD is falling, and we have a report coming out about the Consumer Price Index (CPI), which was predicted to be worse than the previous CPI data. A lot of traders around the world would have shorted this market prior to even seeing the newest released figure as the EURUSD was falling already and the expected figure was to be worse than a prior figure.

Once the new figure came out, and was an even worse number than was expected, even more people would have begun shorting, expecting a further move to the downside. In reality, the opposite happened:

The simple reason that the EURUSD went up instead of down was that there were more buy orders filled than sell orders. Although a generic interpretation would have been that we expected a move to the down-side, perhaps large market players already had clues about the infor-mation and sold much earlier, because the news was already priced in. Alternatively, perhaps there were other indirect forces that motivated the large market players to buy the euro and they simply used this report to purchase large quantities of the euro at a lower price.

We do not know, nor would we ever be able to find out but, what we know for sure is, there were more buy orders than sell orders. It simply could not be otherwise.

Think of buying and selling like anything else in life, let's say a property. If someone is trying to sell a property and no one is buying, after a while the seller needs to lower the price to find a buyer. Once the seller lowers the price, perhaps a buyer emerges, and the transaction takes place, and the "order is filled". If someone wants to buy a property of a certain specification for a set price, and all properties that meet the buyer's specifications are more expensive, he or she may need a budget increase to be able to buy the property.

With the euro, price was falling because there were many sellers and few buyers. For the euro to turn and go back up, it needed to be that there were few sellers and many buyers. At some point in that region of price where the euro turned, large market players would be buying so much from anyone who wanted to sell, to a point where everyone who wanted to sell had sold and there was no longer a significant number of sellers at any of the above price points. Therefore, price had nowhere else to go but up.

What may seem counterintuitive, but is a fact about price movement, is that price does not move because of excess buying or excess selling. Price movement happens because of lack of buying or lack of selling. In the case of a huge market like the euro, how could we end up with a lack of selling, especially in the case of news reports that are likely to encourage sellers? The answer is because the large market players purchased so much that they removed the sellers, so price moves up looking for the next available seller, like how the price of anything moves in real life.

CHARACTERISTICS OF DIRECT FORCES

Movement occurs when orders change status from Un-Filled to Filled, no matter the reason why those orders entered the market in the first place. Having a way to identify those Un-Filled Orders (UFOs) before they get filled would allow a trader to capture market movements without any sort of subjectivity. No "interpretation" would be needed. We don't know why the orders are there and we don't need to know; we simply need to know the objective fact that they are there.

There are small pockets of Un-Filled Orders in the markets that could cause price to pause for a while or cause a small movement in the market. As traders, we want to focus on the larger quantity of orders that are likely to cause bigger and faster movements in the markets. The benefit of this is that once a bigger and faster movement occurs, other traders are likely to join the party and continue to add orders that facilitate that move.

For example, if there is a big stack of buy orders that pushes price up, and then price goes up quickly, traders all over the world may now start buying because they see price going up. Their orders now contribute to price continuing to rise.

This benefits us hugely if we entered at the origin of that move with the initial stack of Un-Filled Orders. For us to make profits, we need others to buy after we buy and push price upwards or sell after we sell and push price downwards.

The question is, "How do we identify UFOs?" To do this, it implies the use of advanced trading technology. Certainly, for people who are experienced and skilled in visually analyzing a chart and finding orders, they could perform this task using their eyes. However, we want to be as mechanical as possible, removing the possibility for human error as much as we can, and basing our trading decisions on objective data, not subjective interpretation.

Additionally, there is more to price than what the human eye can see. It is not just about the structure of the candles that gives us clues about where orders may lie, but information such as volume and the number of trades that took place per candle. These are processes the human eye cannot see and, although we could access that information and analyze it all manually, that would take a long time, and there is still a possibility of error and misinterpretation.

This is why we use technology, which can access the needed information, analyze it and display it to us as trading opportunities, all at the speed of light.

If you were to use the AutoClimate™ app and see that a market is going in a particular direction, and that it is likely to continue to move in that direction, and you know you have UFOs also pointing in the same direction, then it makes a lot of sense to enter at that price. In this case, we have multiple parameters pointing to the same conclusion, which increases the probability of success.

Of course, sometimes orders are canceled and sometimes indirect forces may cause crazy movements in the markets; that's why we use stops. Although we have higher probability, it still isn't guaranteed so we always, always, always use stops.

Huge orders that enter the market from large market players are placed within a range of price, so rather than having a huge order for one exact price point, they will add many orders which are at random prices with random quantities within a range of price. Sometimes tricks are played on retail trades, where market makers will show a very large order at a price point, only for it to be removed at the speed of light just as retail traders start adding their orders.

Very large market players spend incredible amounts of money to locate their super-fast computers and servers in the same buildings and floors as exchanges. The proximity means that the fiber optics that connect the computers to the servers have a nanosecond of extra time than if they were farther away. In the modern technological world, they can play games with this extra time, placing large orders and canceling them to create impressions that price is about to move in a certain direction, encouraging novice buy and sell orders, only to cancel the orders and, perhaps, trade in the opposite direction.

The good news is, when a large market player enters a market, even if they break their order into smaller pieces within a range, they will move price. They can do this because they have enough money for their buy orders to surpass the amount of sell orders or vice versa. The

AutoUFOs® app, which we use as our tool to identify UFOs, is constantly looking for traces that reveal institutional action.

Using technology that points out where the orders are is much more objective; we don't need to care if orders are there for manipulation purposes or from news or, because of unemployment numbers. We only care about understanding the climate and the probability of the market going up or down and then entering the market where big stacks of orders are waiting to move price.

This type of process needs to run in real time, as UFOs can be added or subtracted from a market at any moment in time. As traders, we also need to be ready for that; sometimes you may put on a trade, everything seems to be lining up, all the rules are met, and then a new UFO shows up because new orders are added or one that was there before disappears because orders were canceled. This can lead to a change in the climate too, so you should cancel the trade or plan another trade in the opposite direction.

DIRECT FORCES IN ACTION

Using the same chart of the EURUSD as we used before, we will now show what the AutoUFOs® app would have shown at the time, showing us where Un-Filled Orders were waiting to push price up (in this case). To recap, we had a report at 10:00 a.m. GMT, which was expected to report bad news and, then, when it was released, it actually reported even worse news. From this bad news, many people would expect the market to drop so many novice traders around the world would have gone short (or sold) the euro around this time. We now have UFOs on the chart showing us where Un-Filled Orders would have been:

Important EUR News about to be released at 10:00 AM GMT:
- The EUR is falling ahead of the Report

When "no one" Buys at the current price, but there is a lot of Buying at a lower price, the Market moves down until it finds those Buy Un-Filled Orders (UFOs)

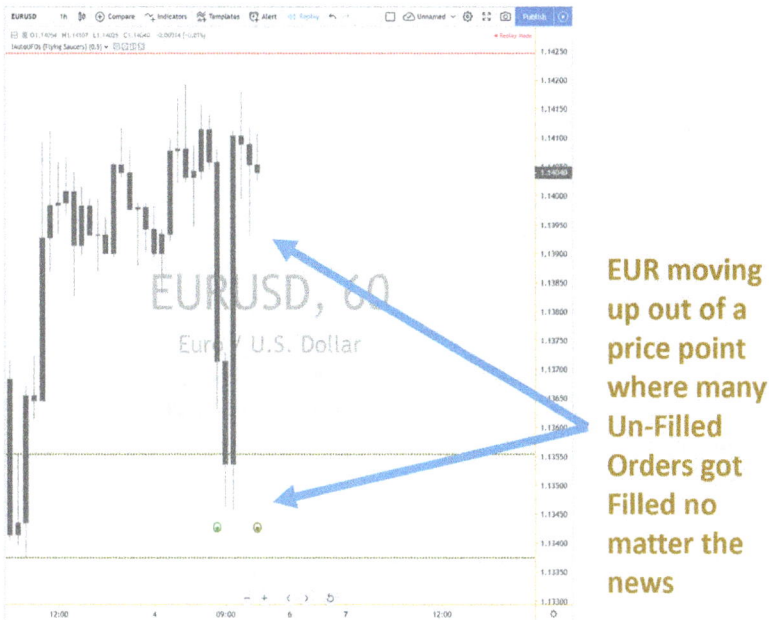

EUR moving up out of a price point where many Un-Filled Orders got Filled no matter the news

This shows us price moving in the opposite direction to what would be expected because there was a big enough stack of buy orders that could create a vacuum of sellers, leading to the only thing that could happen: price went up.

This is the difference between understanding market mechanics or not. A good comparison might be if we talk about architects. If you are not an architect and you look at a particular building, you may be mesmerized by it, and think "how does it stay up?!" If you were the architect, you look at the building and you would see what went into it: the measurements, the physics of gravity, the technology used to calculate everything, etc. The architect would not be mesmerized as he or she would simply see what was expected given the architect's understanding of physics.

Traders might see people on the news, or know other traders, who are surprised or amazed about what is happening in the markets. We see order flow and understand what is going on.

Within the markets, we could categorize traders into predators and prey. Ideally, we'd want to be the ultimate predators, to ensure our survival but that's not possible for retail or individual traders. Our goal as traders is to simply not become prey. We want to enter the market in ways where we benefit from a situation based on probabilities and, if we were to get hurt, we make sure we can survive (stop losses). If you become prey, then you are eaten and cannot survive in the markets.

In other words, when buying and selling, it is key that we buy only when large market players buy and sell only when large market players sell. By aligning our orders with the orders of whoever has the power to move the market, we put probabilities in our favor and increase our likelihood of survival. Using technology that looks for large stacks of orders increases the probability that we are joining the large market players and we are less likely to be prey.

COMBINING FORCES

Despite the fact that Un-Filled Orders ultimately drive price movement, it is important to understand and be aware of the current Market Climate (environment).

Changes in the market environment may lead to UFOs being added to or removed from a market. This is especially true since the markets became electronically traded, meaning that millions of computers worldwide run processes that identify certain real-time conditions and will place or cancel trades/orders based on those setups automatically. The use of advanced trading technology is critical to be objectively in sync with what the markets have to offer.

Ideally, we want to combine direct forces with indirect forces. If you were to pick one, then direct forces are the key, but using them both adds more probabilities in our favor.

Previously we showed an example where if you were to use AutoUFOs® instead of following a news report, you would have had a better chance of catching a profitable move. The AutoUFOs® provided us with objective evidence that a trade could work out. It is not a guarantee, but evidence equals probabilities. So AutoUFOs® put more probabilities in our favor.

Using the same chart as before, we will show you how combining forces gives us good probabilities as well:

JAN 4, the News is about to be reported...
We do nothing and instead we wait to see evidence of new Un-Filled
Orders (UFOs) entering the Market which will confirm the "interpretation"
of the various Indirect forces (from the larger Market players)

GMT	Time left	Event		Vol.	Actual	Consensus	Previous
		FRIDAY, JAN 04					
10:00	✓	■EUR Consumer Price Index - Core (YoY) (Dec) PRELIMINAR			1%	1%	1%
10:00	✓	■EUR Consumer Price Index (YoY) (Dec) PRELIMINAR			1.6%	1.8%	1.9%

Newly added
Buy Un-Filled
Orders (UFOs)

The available Indirect forces are leading for
larger Market players to be Buyers of EUR

EUR moving up as
Indirect + Direct
forces together
drive prices higher

A smart
action
would be
to wait for
price to
return
around
1.1414
and Buy
then

More newly added
Buy Un-Filled Orders
(UFOs) supporting a
new trade

This shows how a combination of both direct and indirect forces can work together to drive prices. New orders were added to the market to the upside, giving us a new opportunity to enter the market that is being pushed up, and entering along with large market players. Another example below:

FEB 1, the same News is about to be reported. Let's do it again!
We do nothing and instead we wait to see evidence of new Un-Filled Orders (UFOs) entering the Market which will confirm the "interpretation" of the various Indirect forces (from the larger Market players)

GMT	Time left	Event		Vol.	Actual	Consensus	Previous
		FRIDAY, FEB 01					
10:00	✓	EUR Consumer Price Index - Core (YoY) (Jan) PRELIMINAR			1.1%	1.0%	1.0%
10:00	✓	EUR Consumer Price Index (YoY) (Jan) PRELIMINAR			1.4%	1.4%	1.6%

Newly added
Sell Un-Filled
Orders (UFOs)

The available Indirect forces are leading for larger Market players to be Sellers of EUR

OTHER TYPES OF INDIRECT FORCES

Moving Averages are technical indicators that are regularly used by fund managers that want to add more to a position and, therefore, they tend to act as an indirect force that adds new UFOs to a market. Moving Average indicators show us an average of price over various periods of time and, as the name implies, they move with price as they calculate price data in real time to show the average price.

Moving Averages may be used by themselves and may produce successful results; however, they are an indirect force that can lead to more orders being added to a position, (or not). The higher probability comes in combining these with the direct force of UFOs in the market.

The use of the Exponential Moving Average (EMA) indicator is often shown on a chart as a line that moves with and through price. Many times, price will come to the EMA-line and move away, then return to the EMA-line and move away again. This isn't always the case; sometimes price moves through the EMA-line but then repeats the same cycle of coming to the EMA-line and moving away.

In the image below, we see that price often moves through the Moving Average when there are no UFOs there to stop it. When combined with a UFO, price indeed, does bounce from the EMA more efficiently:

Moving Average lining up perfectly with a price point with Buy Un-Filled Orders (UFOs)

Price going through the Moving Average as Indirect forces may or may not impact the Market

The GBP bounced nicely and precisely from the Moving Average as Indirect + Direct forces created a powerful synergy

There are many technical traders who would look at this move and assume that the Moving Average alone was responsible, concluding that the average worked very well. The reason it worked so well was because, at the same time, there were UFOs that pushed price up too. We don't know which of those forces was the greatest in this example; it may be that the Moving Average encouraged more new buy orders from fund managers and technical traders, or it may be that the UFO alone pushed price up. However, the odds were greater for a move to the upside because we had both of these forces working towards the same thing.

Fibonacci Retracements are mathematical ratios that are regularly used by traders attempting to identify key price points where to buy or sell and, therefore, could act as an indirect force that adds new UFOs to a market.

The original mathematical theory comes from an Italian mathematician born in 1170, named Fibonacci. He came up with a sequence that is made from taking two numbers and adding them together, then using the answer and the prior number to give the next answer and so on:

0, 1, 1, 2, 3, 5, 8, 13, 21, 34, 55, 89, 144 ...

0+1=1 and 1+1=2 and 1+2=3 and 2+3=5, and so on.

Further to that, if you take any two of those consecutive numbers and divide them, you will get the same ratio. For instance, if you divide 34 by 55 or 89 by 144, you get 0.618, which is known as the "golden ratio".

This ratio can be seen in much of nature and is one of the reasons why Fibonacci's sequence is so famous and also used by some traders, who believe this sequence carries significance in the financial markets as well.

When it comes to Fibonacci Retracements, this golden ratio is used as the basis for other ratios that calculate how far price has moved relative to a prior move. The ratios that are commonly used are: 23.6%, 38.2%, 61.8%, 78.6% and – although it's not technically based on Fibonacci – 50%.

If a stock goes up by $10, the Fibonacci Retracement lines will plot these ratios on the chart relative to that $10 move – at $2.36 into the move, at $3.82 in, at $5.00, at $6.18 and at $7.86.

Those who use Fibonacci Retracement indicators will often point to a beginning of a move and then to an end of a move (for example, a high and low of a candle) and then plot the Fibonacci percentage ratios between those two points. They are expecting that price will react to these areas: if price comes back to the 23.6% retracement, they expect it to bounce from there, if not at the 38.2% line, and so on.

Fibonacci may have an impact on the markets because it is present in nature and, therefore, impacts other phenomena as well. Many programs run by automated computers at a very high institutional level also use Fibonacci in their programming; maybe Fibonacci has an impact because computer programs use it and it becomes a self-fulfilling prophecy. In either case, they can encourage orders to come into the markets.

As with Moving Averages, they are an indirect force, so by themselves they may produce successful results, but when combined with the direct force of UFOs, the probability is higher. The example below shows us how this could work:

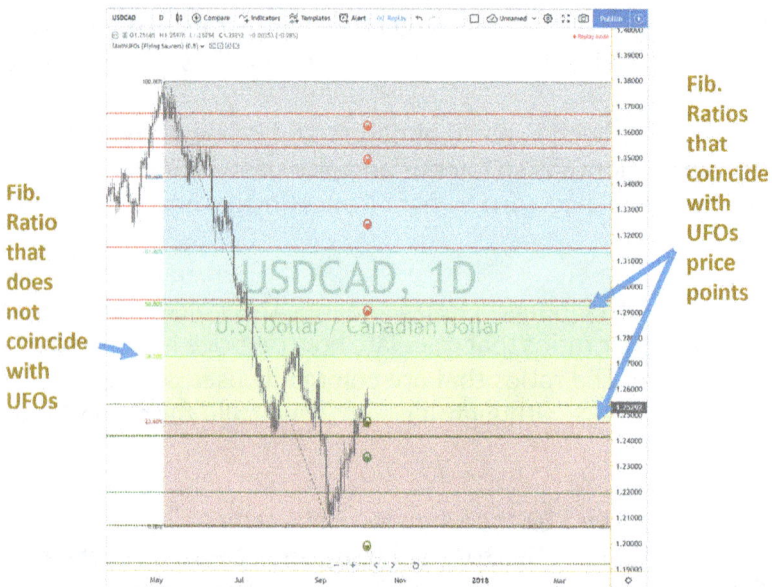

Fib. Ratio that does not coincide with UFOs

Fib. Ratios that coincide with UFOs price points

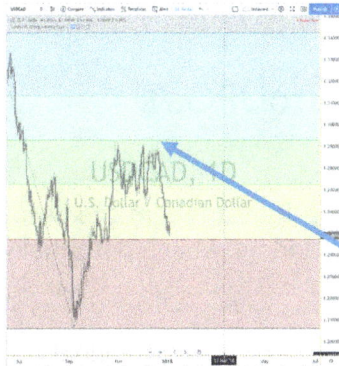

Empowering Fibs retracements and creating a powerful synergy by combining them with UFOs:
- Go Short at the 50%
- Go Long at the 23.6%

Notice how ignoring the 38.2% Fib. retracement was a smart choice. Price went through it effortlessly as only Indirect forces where present there (no UFOs)

In this example, the 38.2% retracement line did not have any Sell UFOs on the chart and price went straight through the line. At the 50% Fibonacci retracement line, there was a Sell UFO present. When price came to that line, it hit a direct selling force from the UFOs, as well as an indirect selling force from the Fibonacci retracement that likely encouraged more sell orders to be added. We don't know if the Fibonacci retracement by itself caused the sell orders to be enough to push price down or the UFO by itself, but it is logical to conclude that the two forces together gave us greater probability of this outcome.

The methodology we will be covering in this book will use mainly the EMA as our indirect force. If we have the climate in our favor, and UFOs combined with indirect forces, we are adding many probabilities to our trades. This is still not guaranteed, so of course we always, always, always use stops.

AutoUFOs®

AutoUFOs® is a Trading App that answers the second question we should be asking ourselves as traders: what is potentially an ideal Buying Price or Selling Price?

Once the market climate is defined and the ideal buying and selling prices are identified, a trader can plan trades knowing when to enter them and when to exit them, maximizing profits when right, controlling losses when wrong and minimizing the number of cases when wrong.

From this point of view, trading is quite simple. It doesn't need to be complicated. We need to understand if the market is presenting a probable opportunity or not and, if so, make a plan, where if we're right we profit nicely and, if we're wrong, we lose small.

Direct forces of buy and sell orders are going to be our ally and the AutoUFOs® app is showing us on a chart where these stacks of large orders are likely to be. The app shows us the orders by displaying either:

A red flying saucer with a red band for sell orders or a green flying saucer with a green band for buy orders

The flying saucers show us where the "meat" of those UFOs is or where the higher number of orders is concentrated. On the right-hand side of the UFO, we see price labels which give us the price information for the range in which the orders are present.

The UFOs are displayed slightly differently depending on whether you are using MetaTrader or TradingView.

On TradingView, the bands are shown as dotted lines in their respective color, with white space between them, and the prices are shown on the price axis on the right-hand side of the chart:

On MT5, the bands are still shown as dotted lines in their respective color, with white space between them, but the relevant prices are shown directly next to the UFO on the chart itself and are not displayed on the price axis.

Buy UFOs are always green but they are displayed in two different shades:

Pure Green = higher concentration of orders and therefore higher probability

Olive Green = lower concentration of orders and therefore lower probability

The sell UFOs are always red but they are also displayed in two different shades:

Pure Red = higher concentration of orders and therefore higher probability

Maroon Red = lower concentration of orders and therefore lower probability

We will use both shades as both highlight a significant number of orders but, if you were a more conservative trader, you may wish to only use those that have higher concentrations of orders and therefore higher probabilities.

The way we use AutoUFOs® is as the answer to Question No. 2, "Where is the ideal buying price and where is the ideal selling price?". We don't simply use them to buy and sell without first having answered Question No. 1: "Should I be a buyer, seller or not trade at all?" Once AutoClimate™ has answered that question for us, we then use AutoUFOs®, combined with the indirect force of the EMA, to give us our buying or selling prices.

Let's say the AutoClimate™ showed us a confirmed upwards climate. We would look for green UFOs that lined up with the EMA for our long entry price. If the AutoClimate™ showed us a confirmed downwards climate, then we would look for red UFOs that lined up with the EMA for our short entry price.

Here is an image showing more about AutoUFOs®:

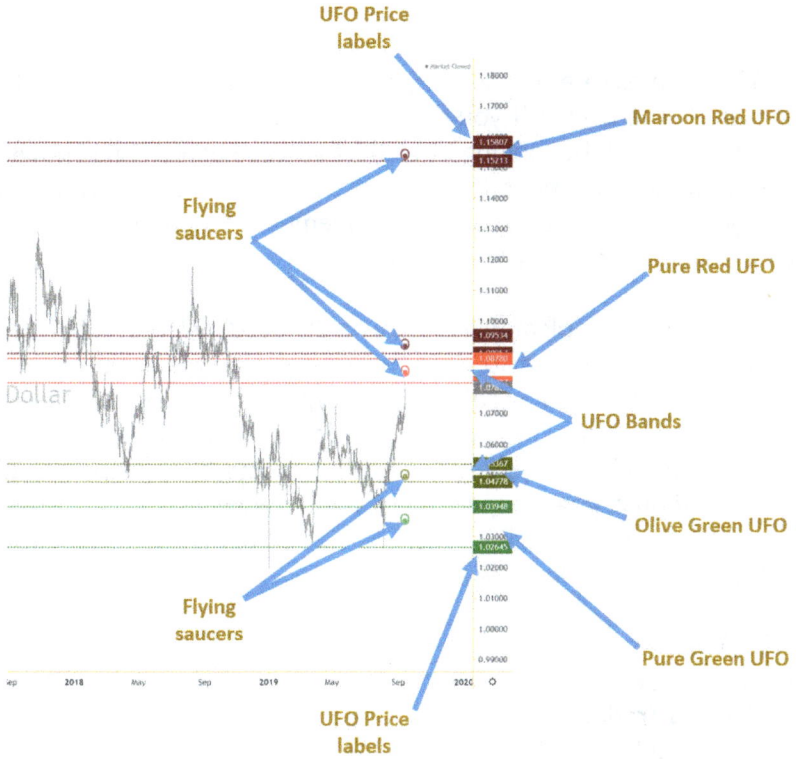

TIMEFRAMES AND STYLES

Chart Timeframes refer to the lifespan of each candle on a chart and can be chosen by the trader. If you choose to view a 60-minute timeframe chart, then you will be looking at a chart where each candle shows 60 minutes of price movement. If you choose to view a monthly chart, then each candle shows a month of price movement. As traders, we choose which timeframes we want to look at.

The timeframes we look at will mostly be dictated by the style of trader we want to be. This is also determined by us as individual traders. Usually, the style of trading refers to the type of trades placed based on their desired duration. However, our choice as to which style of trader we want to be will also depend on other aspects, such as personality, availability of time, goals, capital and risk tolerance.

Common styles of trading are as follows:

- INTRADAY Trader
- SWING Trader
- POSITION Trader
- Long-term INVESTOR

A common mistake that a lot of traders make is to learn a methodology – whether from a course, a book or online – and simply copy it exactly. What if that book was designed for intra-day traders and that doesn't suit your goals or match your personality or time availability? Then you will be forcing yourself to trade way out of your comfort zone, which will have a direct impact on your mindset and, therefore, your performance.

It is important that you identify the style that suits you best before pursuing a methodology. Most of the time, a trader will need to practice a methodology in his or her chosen style in a simulated account for a while, to ensure that it works before risking real money. We would suggest that you practice in this way and that you don't need to decide immediately what style of trader you want to be. Practice the one that makes the most sense for you. If you practice and realize that it's not working for you – for example, you don't have the time to enact the methodology as well, or it's putting you under too much or not enough pressure – you can then practice the methodology using another style to see if that changes things for you.

Your trading style dictates which timeframes you should use. Larger timeframes produce longer-lasting trades and lower timeframes generate trades of a much shorter duration.

For example, if you trade using a weekly timeframe, that will force your trade to be of a long duration and it may take months, or years, for a trade to open and either profit or lose. If you use a one-minute timeframe, then your trade could take a matter of seconds or minutes to close. You could apply the same analysis and act the same but the change in timeframe would change the duration of the trade.

This is a very subjective decision to be made as to which timeframes to use and which style of trader you want to be. Let's say you wish to trade as a secondary income; you love your job and you have no intention of leaving, you just want extra income. In this case you would want your trading routine to be compatible with your other commitments and would therefore use different timeframes than someone who wants to trade as their main income, maybe isn't working and, therefore, has more time. You may be someone who trades multiple styles together, perhaps intra-day trading for quicker income and long-term investing for your retirement. It is entirely subjective.

INTRA-DAY TRADERS

Goal	Capture rapid market moves and be out quickly
Duration	Trades last mins/hours and never more than one day
Philosophy	Not looking for incredible trades, but instead aiming to execute one or more reasonable trades each day
Amount of time spent trading	Up to two hours per session (typical)
Trade Size	Large size is required and therefore trading on margin (leverage) is common
Typical Instruments	Forex, Futures and CFDs
Advantages	Can be done with limited capital
Challenges	Emotions are easily impacted by fast action

As the trades last for a shorter duration, this implies a higher volume of trades. Intra-Day Traders are not looking for the trade of the year as they plan to be out of their trades by the end of the trading day and, therefore, are not looking to catch amazing moves that may last weeks or months. As the moves are smaller, getting paid well requires large sizes; this often leads to the use of leverage when placing these types of trades. However, being in and out of the markets quickly means that margin requirements from many brokers are often less and, therefore, trades can often be executed with more limited capital. We will cover margin and leverage in more detail later in the book.

Here's how you might apply our methodology to an Intra-Day Style:

Different Time-Frames

Same Values

Defined Climate

In this example, the highest timeframe used is a 60-minute chart and we see a thick blue dot (a confirmed upwards climate) with an EMA price at 106.654. We then use the 8-minute chart to find buy (green) UFOs for entry that will envelop the EMA number.

The result of this trade was a 14-pip profit to the upside, which was realized after just over two hours.

The idea is not to trade a hundred times a day, although that would be possible, because that would almost certainly entail a huge psychological impact. Whatever our style, the aim is to prioritize the quality of our trades, not the quantity.

SWING TRADERS

Goal	Allow some time to capture longer market movements
Duration	Trades last multiple hours/days or a few weeks
Philosophy	Looking to secure significant moves that justify overnight risk while running multiple trades in parallel
Amount of time spent trading	Up to two hours per day (typical)
Trade Size	Smaller size is required and therefore trading on margin (leverage) is optional
Typical Instruments	Forex, Options and CFDs
Advantages	Multiple trades in parallel add diversification
Challenges	More complex than managing one trade at a time

The main difference between Intra-Day and Swing Trading is the amount of time it takes to be in and out of a trade. As a Swing Trader, some trades may take weeks before they either hit a target or a stop-loss. Usually, Swing Traders will have more than one trade on at the same time; one of the primary reasons for this is because trades take a bit longer to play out. If you are in one trade and it takes two weeks to stop out before you get into another trade, it can feel like a waste of time and impact your trading psychology. However, if you run multiple trades in parallel, you may have a couple of losses and a couple of profits within a couple of weeks and, overall be at a profit, or incur a smaller loss within the same time period, which is easier to manage psychologically.

Running multiple trades in tandem can incur an extra level of complexity in the sense that it would be unwise to execute multiple correlated trades at the same time. In the case of FOREX, if you go long on the EURUSD and the AUDUSD and the GBPUSD, you are trading the US Dollar three times so a movement on the dollar could incur a loss or profit on all three of your trades. Although this may be good if it results in multiple profits, the flipside is that you are risking more. So there needs to be extra rules around correlated positions, but this is not a difficult process to execute.

Holding trades overnight or over the weekend can incur extra risk of encountering gaps. Gaps can occur overnight on markets that close every day, or over the weekend for markets that are open 24 hours during the week but close over the weekends. The term "gap" refers to price opening at a different price to the close of the previous candle. For example, a stock is valued at $40.50 by the close of day on Wednesday but opens at $42.30 on Thursday morning. This means it "gapped up" by $1.80 (showing as a jump up on the chart) from the previous day's closing candle to the open of the next day's candle. If a stock was valued at $265.30 at the close of the day and then valued at $260.10 on the open of the following day, then it "gapped down" by $5.20.

Gaps can occur during market trading hours but that is extremely rare, whereas overnight and over-the-weekend gaps are reasonably common. The risk with gaps is that you may have a stop that manages your risk and gets you out at a predefined loss but, if the market gaps against you, perhaps the stop could not be filled at the desired price and instead you have a greater risk.

For example, you buy a stock at $172.50 with a stop at $170.50 (a risk of $2 per share), and you're triggered into your trade on a Monday, and it is still open by the time the market closes that day. On Tuesday, the market gaps down, and now the stock is valued at $169.50. As the market was closed overnight, no orders could be filled – the price never actually moved through the gap, meaning it was never at $170.50. Your broker will fill your stop order at the best price possible, which in this case is the open on Tuesday at $169.50.

This incurred $1 more risk per share, which in this example is a 50% greater risk than originally desired. This can be exacerbated when trading markets that involve a use of leverage, like Forex.

However, in Forex trading, gaps don't often occur overnight as the market is traded 24 hours a day during the week (Monday through Friday, US time). The gap risk in Forex happens more over the weekend when the market is closed and, therefore, the opening price on Monday morning can be different than the closing price on Friday night. To justify the gap risk, swing traders use bigger time frames, which reduces the risk of a gap increasing risk and exposing themselves to moves of a longer duration. The bigger moves justify more the additional risk of gaps.

Here's how you might apply our methodology to a Swing Trade Style:

Different Time-Frames

Same Values

Defined Climate

Entry @ 1.3232

Exit @ 1.3143

Climate Propagating

In this example, the methodology is applied in the exact same way as with the prior Intra-Day Trading example; the only difference is the timeframes. The highest timeframe used is the 240-minute (4-hour) chart and the smaller timeframe is the 21-minute chart (as opposed to 60-minute and 8-minute in the previous example). In this image we see a thick red dot (confirmed down climate) on the 240-minute chart and the EMA number 1.3238. We then look at the 21-minute chart to find sell (red) UFOs that envelop the EMA reference number.

The result of this trade was an 89-pip profit to the downside, which was realized in over four days. The size of the move was greater, as was the time it took to achieve it. The methodology was applied in exactly the same way.

POSITION TRADERS

Goal	Capture significant market movements
Duration	Trades last multiple days/weeks or a few months
Philosophy	Looking to secure significant moves that justify overnight risk while running multiple trades in parallel
Amount of time spent trading	Up to five hours per week (typical)
Trade Size	Smaller size is required and therefore trading on margin (leverage) is optional
Typical Instruments	Forex, Options and CFDs
Advantages	Multiple trades in parallel add diversification
Challenges	More complex than managing one trade at the time

Position Trading is a relaxed and slower-paced version of Swing Trading, using higher timeframes. The goals and philosophy are effectively the same but extended over a slightly longer time period. The same concept applies as to running multiple trades in parallel so you're not waiting weeks to enter a trade and getting "itchy" to place trades for the sake of placing them.

However, a Position Trader wouldn't expect to be extremely busy trading every day and would expect trades to run for a while, collecting returns over the longer term. Because the trades last longer and use higher timeframes, it is more likely that a Position Trader would capture a greater move in his or her trades.

Here's how you might apply our methodology to a Position-Trading Style:

In this example, the methodology is applied in the exact same way as before but the timeframes used are Daily and 55-Minute. We see a thick red dot on the Daily chart, which is the AutoClimate™ app telling us we should look to go short, and we have a red UFO on the 55-Minute chart that envelops the EMA from the daily chart:

The result is a 216-pip profit to the downside, realized in just over two weeks. The size of the move is greater again than the examples before, as well as the length of time in the trade, because the timeframes used are greater.

LONG-TERM INVESTORS

Goal	Capture significant market movements as well as other benefits such as dividends
Duration	Trades last multiple weeks/months or a few years
Philosophy	Looking to build a portfolio of wanted assets where their acquisition timing is not seen as critical
Amount of time spent trading	Up to two hours per week (typical)
Trade Size	Limited size and no margin (leverage)
Typical Instruments	Stocks
Advantages	Very relaxed
Challenges	Shorting is not available

Investing can be seen as "trading", just over a longer time period. The goal is to capture significant market moves, which implies the need to be in the trades for significantly longer than the previous styles, with trades lasting up to multiple years. The biggest difference between a Trader of any style and an Investor is the philosophy of building a portfolio where the timing of the entry to the trade is not seen as critical.

Let's say an Investor buys a stock because he or she believes the company is a good one and should grow over time, and, on top of that, the company pays decent dividends. The Investor is not looking necessarily to time entries and exits exactly, but to capitalize on larger market moves over considerable time periods, and/or gain a return from dividend payouts. So even if the stock goes against the investor, he or she would be collecting dividends, and that's part of the portfolio strategy.

The fact that Investors want to own the asset and potentially capitalize on dividend payouts means that they could choose not to use stops, because they want to own the asset and collect dividends, whatever happens to the value of the stock in the short- or mid-term. This implies that

Investors would never use a margin account for these types of trades; they will not use their brokers' leverage to get into these positions. If they purchase a stock, crypto currency, currency, etc., for investment purposes, then they will use cash accounts and, therefore, the most that can be lost is the value of the product and the amount paid.

For example, if a stock is worth $50 per share, then the most that can be lost is $50 per share purchased, if no stops were used and the stock went to $0. If this position was entered into, using a margin account, depending on the level of leverage used, this could result in a larger loss without the use of stops. This is why we always, always, always use stops!

However, if your intention is to own an asset at cash value, benefit from dividends and hold it for the long term, then perhaps your choice would be not to use stops so that you are guaranteed to stay in that investment, continuing to collect dividends, until you choose to close it.

The only way to justify not using stops is not using leverage. It would be a better use of risk management to still use stops and simply apply them in a way where you use bigger timeframes and give yourself a little bit more wiggle room.

Here's how you might apply our methodology to long-term Investing:

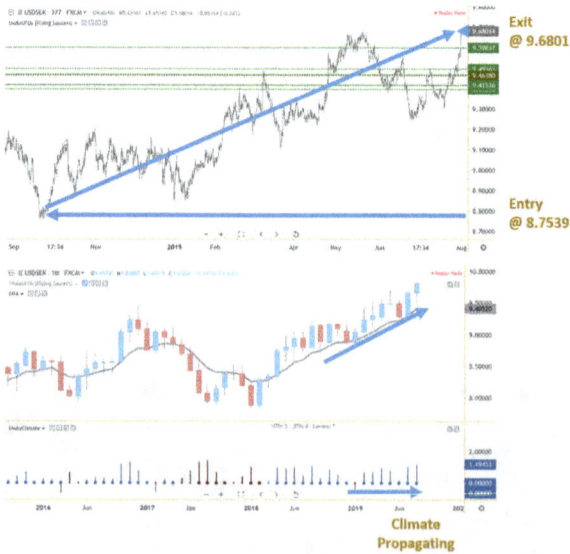

This example shows the exact same application of the methodology but with the larger timeframe as a monthly chart and the smaller timeframe as a 377-minute chart.

The result was a profit of 9,262 pips, collected over 11 months. The size of the move in this example is much greater than previous instances because the trade lasted for much longer, which is due to the larger timeframes used.

However, it is not a usual occurrence for a currency pair to travel over 9,000 pips in a year. The asset used in this example is the US Dollar versus the Swedish Krone, which is more likely to provide these kinds of opportunities than the liquid pairs we mentioned earlier on in the book. Certainly, currency pairs like this one would not be recommended to trade actively because of the lack of liquidity, but may provide longer-term and less precise opportunities.

Hopefully, after exploring the styles of trading in more depth, you will find it easier to identify which style suits you best as an individual, which will in turn dictate the timeframes you use and perhaps the markets you choose to trade.

MULTI-STYLE TRADING

It is common among professional traders to run multiple styles of trading in parallel, as well as combining different instruments. You may have some trades that are position trades in the options markets running passively in your account and, in the meantime, you place some intra-day futures trades or Forex swing trades, and you have some longer-term stocks investments too. This is one example of the combinations available to you as a trader.

There are various benefits to diversifying your trading styles. Firstly, there is no need to force trades because of lack of opportunities. If you look for intra-day trades today and you don't find any quality opportunities, you can still go ahead and search for some swing trades to place, or vice versa, without forcing lower-quality trades for the sake of simply filling time and satisfying the need to place trades.

You can also offset against some markets becoming slow movers. Let's say the EURUSD on the 60-minute timeframe becomes slow and you're in trades for longer than expected; perhaps the 5-minute timeframe is still moving nicely, either on the EURUSD or another market. You can place trades on the smaller timeframes, shortening the time you need to wait to either enter or exit your trades. This means you can expose yourself to diversified assets as well as diversified time exposure in your trades.

We would recommend that to begin with, if trading is new to you, focus on one style that suits you better and hone the skill for that specific application. Then you can expand from there and diversify, if you are inclined to.

RISK EXPOSURE

For a Trading Methodology to be stable, its Trade Risk exposure needs to be as close to constant as possible. Too much variability would tend to produce random results.

Let's say your initial trade risk is $100, then the next trade you place, you risk $200, then the next one is a $50 risk and the next one is $500. Your losses would be inconsistent, and so would your relative profits. Let's assume that in each of these four examples, the trader was aiming for a 2:1 Reward-to-Risk ratio, and the following happened:

- 1st trade risks $100 to make $200 and wins, profit of **$200**
- 2nd trade risks $200 to make $400 and loses, loss of **$200**
- 3rd trade risks $50 to make $100 and wins, profit of **$100**
- 4th trade risks $500 to make $1000 and loses, loss of **$500**
- Overall loss of **$400**

If the risk was kept constant and the risk was always roughly the same (let's say $100), then the same series of events would produce different overall results:

- 1st trade risks $100 to make $200 and wins, profit of **$200**
- 2nd trade risks $100 to make $200 and loses, loss of **$100**
- 3rd trade risks $100 to make $200 and wins, profit of **$200**
- 4th trade risks $100 to make $200 and loses, loss of **$100**
- Overall profit of **$200**

In either case, the Reward-to-Risk ratio was the same, and the percent profitability was the same, but the results were significantly different based on the consistency of the risk value.

Risk is a word that is often misunderstood; the first impression that new traders, or even experienced traders, may have, is that risk is a negative thing. This cannot be the case because with no risk there is also no reward. Assuming risk is the recipe to be exposed to reward.

However, taking heavy risk just for the sake of chasing heavy reward would not be the right way to approach trading either. We need to manage our risk and seek the balance between probability, risk and reward.

As we mentioned at the beginning of this book, we see risk as the amount of money you are willing to pay to see what happens next; in the same way you would be willing to pay to see a movie that may be great or may be terrible. Risk is the amount of money that you are comfortable to pay to see what happens next on your trades and that number should be as constant as possible.

The risk value for any trade comes from its size as well as from the distance between the entry price and the stop-loss price:

$$SIZE \times DISTANCE = RISK\ VALUE$$

The greater the size of the trade, the greater the risk. The greater the distance, the greater the risk

For each trade, you will change the size of the trade to align it with your personal desired risk value, regardless of the distance between entry and stop (which is objective and should not be changed).

Size refers to how much of the product you buy or sell; in the case of Forex, it refers to how much of the currency you are trading. Is it 20,000 Euros, 3,000 Euros, 400,000 Euros, or another value? This could be any amount, decided by you as a trader, and the margin you have in your account. Forex unit size is denominated in what's called "lots," which refers to the size of the trade (the amount of currency used).

The distance between the entry and stop is set by AutoUFOs®, which shows us two prices based on the objective data the app is analyzing. This is not something we can change as traders; to do so would be to ignore objective data and start to place our orders based on random and subjective parameters, which is more likely to lead to inconsistent results.

We use the AutoUFOs® to provide us with our entry and stop values, which will be different for every trade. To keep our risk value constant, the only parameter we can change is the size of the trade.

However, some traders may choose to alter their entry price (and only their entry price, never their stop loss), while still using the data coming from the AutoUFOs®. The inner circles (the flying saucers within the bands) of the UFOs show a higher concentration of orders, so a trader could choose to take their entry based on the inner circles, keeping their stop constant with the numbers provided by AutoUFOs®. This would reduce the notional risk of the trade, but it could lead to missing some good trades.

If price touches the band of the UFO and moves away, having not touched the inner flying saucer, the trader would miss the entry and could therefore miss out on the profits. The stop-loss will always, always, always be in the same location and should never be moved to accommodate an individual trader. If the notional value of the trade is too high, even with the lowest size, simply do not trade and move on to another opportunity.

However, this invokes an approach which is less objective and less consistent. Inconsistent action leads to inconsistent results. We want to rely on the objectivity of technology to identify the key location for price points, instead of doing it manually based on preferences.

Therefore, the best way to adjust your total risk value is not to alter the distance between your entry and stop but to alter your trade size.

Both size and distance impact the risk and the distance is a given, so, the only thing we have left to change the total risk of the trade, is the size. This cannot be done unless we previously define our desired risk value.

DEFINING "DESIRED" RISK

Think about this as the amount of money you are willing to pay to see what happens next in your trades. Of course, we do not "desire" risk; most people would rather avoid it. However, we need to understand that there is no reward without risk so we need to define what we are comfortable with.

Our desired per-trade risk should then be kept as consistent as possible. You will be able to adjust the trade size to make sure the risk per trade equals the desired trade risk value.

It can be difficult, especially for new traders, to decide on their desired trade value: Should it be $10, $100, $5, $2,000? This number will depend on many things.

If you are a very conservative trader you would restrict this number to be smaller than someone who is more naturally a risk-taker. A trader with a larger account size will risk more than someone with a smaller account. A skilled trader may choose to risk more than someone who is newer to the markets. If a trader's results are profitable, they may choose to risk more; if the account is losing, he or she may choose to further restrict the risk.

One way to quantify your trade risk is to use a percentage of your account, where the percentage never exceeds 2% of the total account size. For example, if an account is $10,000, then the risk should never exceed $200 per trade. If the account is $500, then the risk should never exceed $10, and so on.

What is important to consider when deciding what value (up to 2%) you are comfortable risking, is to ensure that whatever this value is, it does not trigger any emotion. Let's say that your account is $10,000 (remember, everyone will have a different account size), and you choose to risk 1% of your account per trade: That means you are risking $100. If you are wrong on a trade, then you lose $100.

Close your eyes and envision this happening, maybe a few times in a row. If you feel okay, that would suggest this is an appropriate number for you. If you are uncomfortable with it, then maybe 1% risk is too much, in this case and it would be better to risk 0.5% or 0.25% instead.

Every individual trader will have a different account size, different risk tolerance and different level of comfort, so the risk number will be different and unique for each. Think about what your account size is and which percentage of that account (up to 2%) you feel comfortable risking per trade, while understanding you may take multiple consecutive losses. Visualize taking a few losses with that amount of capital risked per trade and monitor how you feel so you can choose the number that you are comfortable with. What is the amount you are comfortable to pay to see what happens next with your trades?

Even if you are comfortable risking a lot (relative to your account size), never exceed 2% risk per trade. If you were to risk more than that and go through a series of losers, which can of course happen, you would erode too much of your capital and have to claw back your losses. This invokes more trading emotion, leading to less consistency and objectivity, and therefore less probability of success.

The markets require us to be rational and objective and we are emotional beings as humans. We need to structure our methodology and approach as much as possible to limit the impact of trading emotions and managing risk is one of the most powerful ways to manage our emotions.

A trader starting with a smaller account may be frustrated by keeping their risk at 2% or lower, as the relative reward is a small number and therefore growth will be slow. However, if the trading is consistently profitable, then the account will grow and the same 2% will be worth a higher number.

Patience is crucial for growing a small account. If a trader is impatient and wants to see the account grow very quickly and therefore risks 5%, 10% or 25% per trade, then they only need to be wrong a handful of times in a row before the whole account is gone. This is not a consistent approach to the markets; this would be more like gambling.

After trading and building your skill with a smaller account, you are trading for the sake of doing a good job and not focusing so much on the money. If you are able to do that, and focus on simply executing your trading plan as close to objective as you can, the money is more likely to come naturally. Experience, number of trades, comfort, account size and risk tolerance are all elements that will impact your desired risk per trade. One way to think about it may be the following:

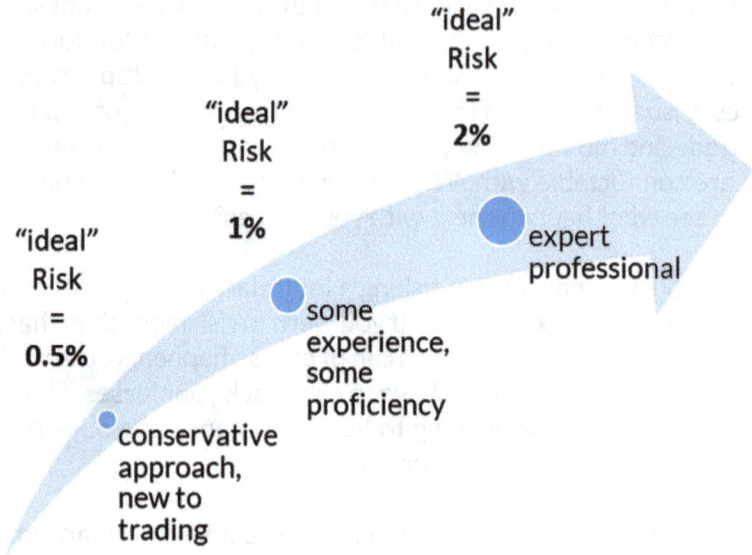

"ideal"
Risk
=
2%

"ideal"
Risk
=
1%

"ideal"
Risk
=
0.5%

expert
professional

some
experience,
some
proficiency

conservative
approach,
new to
trading

Perhaps when you start trading and you're less experienced and less confident, it would be better to risk a smaller amount and then, as you grow and develop your skill, increase your risk incrementally until you are at expert level and then risk the full 2% per trade.

The same is true for the number of trades you take at the same time. If you are executing multiple trades at the same time and you risk 2% for each one and, let's say there is some unexpected market volatility and you get stopped out on all of them, you could end up losing a significant portion of your account quickly, which is likely to trigger emotion. Therefore, it makes more sense to use a smaller risk percentage when you are risking multiple trades at once, and increasing the risk-per-trade if you are only executing one trade at a time (such as when investing).

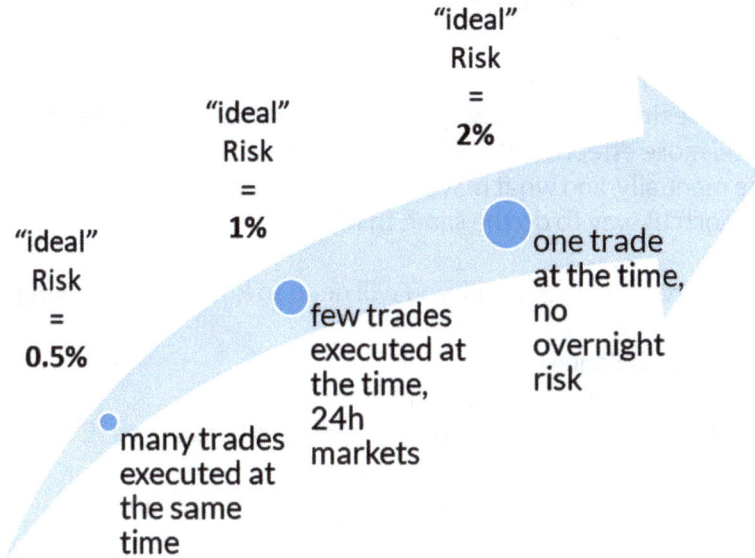

"ideal" Risk = 0.5% — many trades executed at the same time

"ideal" Risk = 1% — few trades executed at the time, 24h markets

"ideal" Risk = 2% — one trade at the time, no overnight risk

The goal is never to surpass 2% and, most importantly, to feel peace when you think about the amount of money you are willing to pay to see what happens next.

If you are uncomfortable with any risk, even $1 and after trading in a demo account, then it would suggest that most probably trading is not for you. We are all unique and sometimes trading just isn't something that suits an individual, just like anything else in life - and that's okay.

We love trading and we love others to learn and share our passion. With practice, courses, even NLP and therapy, people can work on their fear of risk, or whatever is holding them back, and become better traders. But that doesn't mean everybody should do it.

If you are going to trade, then you need to be in a place where you have a level of peace when envisioning your risk, even if you were to lose five times in row. At the same time, you don't want to take too much risk, so follow the rule of not risking more than 2% of your account per trade.

CALCULATING THE RIGHT SIZE

There are two ways of calculating the right size for your trade to make it fit your desired risk. One way is lengthy and tedious and the other is easier and more effective. We will show you both so that you know how it is done manually, and what math goes into the calculation, before knowing the shortcut way to do the same thing.

If you were to do it by hand, you will need to know the following:

- Account Balance (Ab)
- "Desired" Trade Risk Value (R%)
- Distance between the Entry and the Stop Loss prices (ES)
- Minimum Price Fluctuation (mF)
- Multiplier Value for the Min. Price Fluctuation (Mv)

The minimum price fluctuation is different depending on the market traded. Stocks move at a minimum of 0.01, meaning they move up or down one cent at a time. In the Futures markets, they move up and down by a minimum fluctuation that is called a "tick."

When trading the S&P Futures, for example, the tick is 0.25, not 0.01; so every time the S&P futures moves up or down, it moves by 0.25. In Forex, the minimum price fluctuation is called a "pip", which (in most currency pairs) refers to the fourth decimal place (0.0001). In Yen pairs, it refers to the second decimal place (0.01). In either case, it still refers to the smallest price movement.

The Multiplier Value for the Minimum Price Fluctuation refers to how much each of the smallest price movements is worth if trading with the minimum size. In stocks, it is relatively easy because each stock moves up in multiples of 0.01 and each of those movements is worth $0.01 if trading with one share.

In Futures, depending on the market traded, the tick value changes. Sometimes a tick is worth $5, sometimes it is worth $12.50, sometimes $1. This will be dictated by the specific market traded but still refers to the lowest value per tick if traded with one futures contract.

In Forex, the multiplier value refers to how much each pip is worth, otherwise known as "pip value", when traded with 1 micro-lot (which is the smallest size in Forex). This also differs slightly depending on the market.

Once you have the above information, the trade size is calculated using the following formula:

$$Trade\ Size = \frac{Ab \times R\%}{ES \times \frac{Mv}{mF}}$$

Here is an example:

- Account Balance (Ab) → Ab = $10,000
- "Desired" Trade Risk value (R%) → R% = 1% = $100
- Distance between the Entry and the Stop Loss prices (ES) Entry is 1.1212 – Stop is 1.1203 → ES = 0.0009
- Minimum Price Fluctuation (mF) → mF = 0.0001
- Multiplier Value* for the Min. Price Fluctuation (Mv) → is $0.10/pip per micro-lot → Mv = 0.10
- Trade size = $100/ (0.0009 x (0.10/0.0001)) = 111.11... = 11 micro-lots

We always round down what the answer is to ensure that our desired risk is a maximum number and never surpassed.

Here is an example with a Yen Pair:

- Account Balance (Ab) → Ab = $10,000
- "desired" Trade Risk value (R%) → R% = 1% = $100
- Distance between the Entry and the Stop Loss prices (ES) Entry is 139.50 – Stop is 139.22→ ES = 0.28
- Minimum Price Fluctuation (mF) → mF = 0.01
- Multiplier Value* for the Min. Price Fluctuation (Mv) → is $0.10/pip per micro-lot → Mv = 0.10
- Trade Size = $100 / (0.28 x (0.10/0.01)) = 35.71... = 35 micro-lots

The only difference is that, because it is a Yen Pair, the minimum price fluctuation is 0.01 instead of 0.0001. The math is done in the same way, with slightly different inputs, but still allows the trader to understand how many micro-lots they need to use to risk their desired amount ($100).

If you love math, then this is fun and easy for you. If you hate math, then don't worry, you don't actually need to do any of this calculation. We can use technology to calculate the formula for us, which is not only easier, but incurs fewer mistakes. Even if you love math, we would still advise to use the following technology to ensure there is less room for error.

Using TradingView, you can use the Order Panel tool to input your entry, stop and desired risk; it will work out everything else for you. If you click on the Order Panel (usually on the right-hand side, two arrows next to each other, one pointing up, one pointing down), first you need to choose whether you are buying and selling, then fill in the cells as shown: your entry price; stop loss and target prices; and desired trade risk.

Make sure you are looking at the correct market (for example GBPUSD), so that the market you analyzed on the chart is the same market you are calculating the trade size for.

Buy example:

FX:**GBPUSD**, PAPER TRADING	↻ ⚙ ✕
SELL 1.24600	0.4	BUY 1.24604

MARKET | LIMIT | STOP

Order Price

1.24490 ⌄	Ask - 114 ⌄
Absolute	Ticks

Quantity

35 714	▦	100.00	0.10
Units		$ Risk	% Risk

☑ Take Profit   4.93   Stop Loss ☑

138.0	Pips	28.0
1.25870	Price	1.24210
492.85	$	100.00
0.50	%	0.10

Time in Force GTD 17 Sep 2019, 07:20 AM

BUY 35 714 FX:GBPUSD @ 1.24490 LMT

Step #1: Click on BUY

Step #2: Input your Entry Price

Step #3: Input your Stop Loss and Target

Step #4: Input your "desired" Trade risk

Step #5: Round down and use the Units value as the right Trade Size for your Trade

In this instance, TradingView is telling us that to fit within our desired risk for this trade ($100), we need to risk 35,714 units. We would round this down to 35,000 and use 35k in this trade. In the world of Forex, we would refer to that as "35 micro-lots."

TradingView is doing the same calculation that we laid out before; behind the scenes it knows the pip value (multiplier value) and the minimum fluctuation for each currency pair. It then calculates our ES and units from the inputs we provide (our entry, stop and desired risk).

The same calculation is done if we look at a sell example and the inputs we provide are put in the exact same places. The only difference is that you will need to click "sell" instead of buy. This will change a lot of the color scheme to red so that will give you a clue as to whether you've clicked on the correct selection.

Sell example:

Step #1: Click on SELL

Step #2: Input your Entry Price

Step #3: Input your Stop Loss and Target

Step #4: Input your "desired" Trade risk

Step #5: Round down and use the Units value as the right Trade Size for your Trade

In this example, TradingView is telling us that to fit within the $100 desired risk, we must now risk 58,126 units (rounded down to 58,000), which is 58 micro-lots.

TRADING INSTRUMENTS

There are two key groups of instruments:

- **Prime Instruments** = classical assets that may or may not be used for speculation purposes, which vary their value based on the number of buyers and sellers
- **Derivative Instruments** = financial contracts that are linked to a specific underlying asset from which they derive most of their value although other external factors may also play a role in defining their value

A good way to think about the differences between these types of instruments is to picture real estate, as it's a tangible object so it's usually easier to understand. A house or apartment or condo is a prime instrument so you may buy it because you want to live in it, or you may buy it because you wish to speculate on its value and make money from an investment. Therefore, the asset of the house is a prime instrument.

You would also have an insurance policy to protect that asset, like home insurance. The home insurance mainly derives its price from the value of the property; the more expensive the house, the more expensive the home insurance. Certainly, the value of the insurance is linked to the value of the house, but there are other factors that impact the value of the home insurance. For example, if the house is near a flood plain or in a part of the world that is often exposed to natural disasters, then the insurance will likely be more expensive. If the insurance lasts for a year, it will be a different price than if it lasts for a month. There are various factors that also play a role in the price of the insurance. Therefore, the insurance contract is a derivative instrument.

In the real world, you would have to buy the house to speculate on its value, which ties up a lot of capital. In the world of trading, we can buy and sell the derivatives to speculate on the value of the underlying asset. It would be like buying the home insurance policy, waiting for the value of the house to go up and selling the insurance policy to someone else, making a profit out of the difference, without needing to own the house.

In the trading world, these derivative contracts (which are liquid) are the Futures markets, the Options markets and CFDs.

Forex is a prime instrument: we can speculate directly on the currencies, but we can also speculate on Forex through the instruments that derive their value from the currencies.

Stocks are a prime instrument: of course, we can directly trade stocks, or we can trade options on stocks, or single-stock futures.

The following list represents key Prime Instruments:

- Property (real estate)
- Physical Commodities (gold, silver, etc.)
- Fixed Income/Treasuries/Credit
- Funds (mutual funds/unit trusts)
- Stock Shares
- Currencies

The following list represents key Derivative Instruments:

- Futures
- Options
- Credit Derivatives
- CFDs (Contracts for Difference)
- Spread Betting
- Binary Options*

*Binary Options are not to be confused with regulated exchange-traded options.

CURRENCIES

The technical definition of a currency, according to investopedia.com is: "Currency is a medium of exchange for goods and services. In short, it is money, in the form of paper or coins, usually issued by a government and generally accepted at its face value as a method of payment."

You can speculate on the price of currencies in various ways. The Prime instruments used are:

- Cash
- Spot Forex
- Forwards
- Cryptocurrencies

Cash is not efficient as there is no leverage and it's always at risk of physically being lost. Forwards are useful for companies that want to lock in some future exchange rate to purchase products that their company deals in but are not liquid for traders. Cryptocurrencies are more controversial; some argue that there is no intrinsic value in cryptocurrencies but they certainly are a prime instrument that many people buy and sell. Spot Forex is the most liquid and efficient way to trade the currency markets and that is the market we will focus on in this book.

There are also ways to speculate on currency via Derivative Instruments:

- FX CFDs
- FX Futures
- FX Options

CFD stands for "Contract for Difference" – contracts that derive their value from an underlying asset. They are very common in Europe and Asia but are not allowed in the United States. Some Forex brokers outside of the US may market themselves as Forex brokers but, in reality, they are Forex CFD brokers.

Forex Futures and Forex Options are ways to trade currencies in a centralized exchange where every broker will provide the same price.

TERMINOLOGY CORNER

Leverage/Margin

Leverage is a multiplier effect as a consequence of Trading on Margin; where Margin refers to the capital required by brokers (often suggested by Exchanges) in order to be allowed to execute a Trade of a specific Size (notional value). In the case of Forex, it is not Exchanges that set the margin requirements as there is no exchange, therefore, it's the individual brokers who set the margin requirements.

Example:

Buying 100 shares of a stock trading at $225/share would cost $22,500 (notional value) without the use of Leverage

If a broker only required half of this cost for the trade to be allowed, then...

- The Margin would be $11,250
- The Leverage would be 2:1

The margin is how much you need to provide so the broker will allow you to take the trade. This is different from risk. As we covered before, you can size your trade as needed to keep the risk to be whatever you want it to be. Margin simply refers to the capital that your broker requires you to have in your account to allow you to place a trade.

Leverage is the effect of margin. If you need $5,000 to place a trade worth $10,000, then the leverage is 2:1. If you need $5,000 to place a trade worth $100,00, then the leverage is 20:1 and so on.

Margin Call

Investopedia's definition says: "A margin call occurs when the value of an investor's margin account (that is, one that contains securities bought with borrowed money) falls below the broker's required amount. A margin call is the broker's demand that an investor deposit additional money or securities so that the account is brought up to the minimum value, known as the maintenance margin."

If you were in a stock trade that was worth $20,000 (notional value) and the broker required $10,000 to take the trade, and you were to place a trade that went against you so much that your $10,000 had depleted, the broker will ask you to top-up your account – if not, they will close the trade for you. In this example, the stock would need to half in value for this to happen, but if you trade Forex or other markets that provide higher leverage, the product wouldn't have to move too much for a margin call to be issued. If your leverage was 20:1, then the product would only need to move 5% against you for the margin call to be issued.

Although the phrase is "margin call," in reality the margin call comes in the form of an email or pop-up on your platform, letting you know that you need to add more capital to your account to remain in the trade.

We should never find ourselves in a position where we're getting a margin call, because we always, always, always use stops. We will never be in a situation where price goes so badly against us that our brokers issue margin calls against us because we will have stop-losses that get us out at a much smaller, pre-defined loss.

The only situation that we could be in where we get a margin call while using stops is if we have a gap against us. This is more likely to happen in stocks overnight or possibly over the weekend in Forex. The gap could surpass your stop and you cannot get out until the market reopens the next day or on Monday. When the market reopens, if the gap has gone against you, you may suffer a worse risk than you had originally intended.

If you trade liquid markets, this is unlikely to happen. Using smaller position sizes will also minimize this risk, which is more common in swing and position trading.

Bid

Price set by the buyers. This is where Buyers' Limit Orders are waiting to be filled. It signifies where buyers are willing to buy or where they are "bidding" for sellers to sell to them. If you were to enter the market right now with a market order to sell, this is the price you would have to sell to, as that is where the closest buyer is waiting.

Ask

Price set by the sellers. This is where Sellers' Limit Orders are waiting to be filled. It signifies where sellers are willing to sell, or where they are "asking" for buyers. If you were to enter the market right now with a market order to buy, this is the price you would have to buy from, as that is where the closest seller is waiting.

Bid-Ask Spread

Also known as "Spread," this is the difference between the Bid and Ask price. The Bid is always the lower price, and the Ask is always the higher price. The spread can be seen as the cost of going in and out of the market because, if you bought from the Ask now and then immediately sold to the Bid, you would lose the difference between the Bid and Ask prices.

Last

Price at which the Last transaction took place (buyers bought at the Asking Price or sellers sold at the Bidding Price). This is the number we see as "current price" on our price axis on our charts (with centralized markets).

These terms are important in the world of trading, but not just in financial markets; these apply to everything in life. A great example is real estate. There is a price that the seller wants to sell for (or what they "ask" for); buyers will offer their prices that they're willing to buy for (or their "bids"), which are often lower than the seller's ask price. Either the buyer increases the bid to the seller's Ask, or the seller reduces the price to the buyer's Bid, or there is a deal in between. Then the transaction takes place, giving a final value for the property (the Last price). This is how it works in the world of the financial markets as well.

The Bid and the Ask, and therefore the Bid-Ask Spread, is present in every financial market, but it works slightly differently depending on the asset class. As we delve further into Spot Forex mechanics, we will see how it works with Forex.

SPOT FOREX MECHANICS

CURRENCY PAIRS

Currencies can be traded by themselves using derivative instruments but, in the spot market, we need to put them together. The trading of currencies is done by putting two currencies together, where one is bought in exchange for selling the other one.

MAJORS

Most liquid Pairs with the US Dollar in them: EUR/USD, GBP/USD, AUD/USD, NZD/USD, USD/JPY, USD/CHF, USD/CAD

MINORS

Less liquid Pairs with no USD in them (some exceptions such as USD/SGD). These can also be referred to as "cross pairs": GBP/CAD, EUR/AUD, CHF/JPY

BASE VS. QUOTE

Each currency pair has a "base" and a "quote". The Quote Currency measures how much of it is needed to obtain one unit of the Base Currency; in other words, the Base Currency is priced using the Quote Currency. The Base is the first currency in the pair, the Quote is the second currency.

Example:

- EURUSD trading at 1.1010 means that it would take $1.1010 to obtain 1€
- The EUR is the Base Currency
- The USD is the Quote Currency

Pip

This stands for Percentage In Points. It is the minimum price increment based on the FX conventions. We find a Pip in the fourth decimal place (0.0001) in most Currency Pairs, but in the second decimal place (0.01) in Pairs with the JPY. For example, if we looked at NZDUSD and saw the price is 1.6559, then the digit "9" is the pip. If we looked at GBPJPY and saw the price is 139.62, then the digit "2" is the Pip.

It is common to use quotes with fractional Pips, which imply one additional digit (5 for most Pairs, 3 for JPY Pairs). For example:

EURUSD travelling from 1.10100 to 1.10180 represents an 8-Pip move

EURUSD travelling from 1.10158 to 1.10247 represents an 8.9-Pip move

EURJPY travelling from 118.888 to 119.813 represents a 92.5-Pip move

The last digit in all currency pairs, JPY or otherwise, refers to one-tenth of a Pip. They were originally brought into Forex markets to allow brokers to charge commissions that could be smaller than a Pip. As traders, we focus on the fourth decimal place (or second with JPY pairs) and use those digits for our buying and selling references.

Lots

This refers to the units used to trade the currencies or the trade size. In US stocks, the trade is sized in shares; in Futures and Options, the trade is sized in contracts; in Forex, the trade is sized in multiples of lots, and this is set by FX conventions. There are three types of Lots that define the size of our trades:

- Standard Lots = Otherwise referred to as STD-Lots or simply "lots." This is worth 100,000 of the base currency. For example, if you were to trade one lot of the GBPUSD, then you are trading £100,000. If you are trading two lots on the USDCAD, then you are trading $200,000. When we start placing orders in MT5 (trading platform), we won't need to type "100,000" or "200,000" – we just type in "1" as it refers to one lot, or "2" as it refers to two lots.
- Mini Lots = This is a way to trade a smaller size. Mini-lots are valued at one-tenth the size of a standard lot, and refer to 10,000 of the base currency. If you trade four "minis" of the EURUSD, then you are trading €40,000. In MT5, one mini-lot is referred to as "0.1"
- Micro Lots = This is an even smaller trade size. Micro-lots are valued at one-tenth the size of a mini-lot and refer to 1,000 of the base currency. On MT5, one "micro" is referred to as "0.01"

Example:

- "I am long 35 minis of EURAUD" = €350,000 trade size
- "I am short six lots of NZDUSD" = NZ$600,000 trade size
- "I am long 58 micros of GBPJPY" = £58,000 trade size

Pip Value

This refers to the specific monetary impact that a one-Pip move on a Currency Pair would produce in the Trader's account. Pip-Values depend on which currencies are part of the pair as well; specifically, which currency is funding the Trading Account. Pip-Values also depend on the number of Lots (Trade Size).

If you have your trading account in US dollars and place a trade where you buy the EURGBP at 1.1050 and it goes up to 1.1065 (a 15-Pip move), the Pip value will let you know how much that 15-Pip move was worth to you in USD. If you have an account in a different currency, then the pip-value will let you know how much that 15-Pip move was worth in your account's currency.

If your account is in USD and you buy the EURGBP, this implies a double conversion. The Pip value is shown in your account currency, so if the Pip value of the EURGBP is $0.13 then the smallest movement up or down on the EURGBP (trading one micro-lot) is worth 13 cents to a US-based trader. If they traded four micro-lots, then a Pip is worth $0.52. If they trade 20 mini-lots, then a Pip is worth $26, and so on.

It can be tedious to calculate this all manually and, of course manual processes come with greater probability of human error and mistakes, so we use Pip calculators or technology to calculate the Pip value. We use TradingView to easily calculate this value, which will show under "Order Info" at the bottom of the order panel.

TradingView will take into account the lots (or units) used, the Currency Pair traded and the Currency in the account. It will show us what the smallest move in this Currency Pair is worth to us as Traders. If we changed the number of units traded (lots), then the Pip value would show as a different number.

Another example of how Pip values are calculated:

EURUSD travelling from 1.10100 to 1.10180 represents an 8-Pip move Trade Size is 45 Micros and the Pip-Value is $0.10/Pip per Micro-Lot Therefore the $ Profit is $36 (Eight Pips x $0.10/Pip x 45 Micros)

Non-Centralized Market

When we trade markets like stocks, we have data feeds loading into our charts, coming from an exchange, so every broker will show the same pricing. The current price that we see on the chart is always the "Last" price.

In the Spot Forex Markets there is no exchange but, instead, an interbank system, so trades are being filled in different banks. Because of the nature of Forex and the decentralized structure, this implies some key consequences to be kept in mind:

- Different Platforms may show slightly different quotes
- Most Forex Charts display the Bid Price, not the Last Price, the way it would happen with centralized markets
- Both of these consequences are reasons for:
- Adding additional distance to Stop Loss locations (extra wiggle room)
- Increasing the Buying Price to avoid missing fills (Ask Prices are always higher than the Bid Prices)

Because there will be various prices being traded, depending on which banks and brokers are being used, there cannot be a "Last" price in Forex. Brokers usually show the bid price on their charts. This has an impact because, when you buy, you buy from the Ask, not from the Bid. The Ask is always higher than the Bid, so any Buy orders you place (either Entries or Stops) need to be higher than the price you see on the chart, to increase likelihood of being filled.

Example:

- **Long Trade** = prices on the chart show to buy at 110.10, stop (sell order when Long) at 110.05 (risk 5 Pips). In reality, you may buy at 110.12 in order to buy from the Ask, with your stop at 110.00, to give yourself a bit of wiggle room. The risk is now 12 Pips.
- **Short Trade** = prices on the chart show to sell at 120.60, stop (buy order when Short) at 120.75 (risk 7 Pips). As you sell to the bid, your entry would remain the same at 120.60, but your stop has to take into account wiggle room and the necessity to buy from the Ask (not the bid). Therefore, the stop may become 120.82, so the risk is now 14 Pips.

It would be problematic if you didn't know about this in the Forex markets: you would be more likely to see that you'd be stopped out (take a loss) then see price go your way, because you didn't give the stop the wiggle room it needs, or you didn't buy from the Ask. If traders see this happen frequently, they are more likely to get frustrated and therefore change or break their rules, which makes their actions less consistent, leading to their results being less consistent.

It could be equally true that traders end up missing some good long trades because they are not buying from the Ask and, therefore ,miss out on good profits, which can be frustrating and once again lead to breaking or changing rules.

The above is true for any decentralized market, like CFDs and Cryptocurrencies, as well as Spot Forex.

COMMISSIONS

There are two main ways Brokers charge transaction fees in Forex:

- **Commissions per trade** = the broker gives you raw spreads and better routing but to do that charges a commission based on the size of the trade
- **Widening the Bid-Ask Spread** = There is no commission, but the spread will be wider

Pro Accounts are normally commission-based and tend to offer much better Bid-Ask Spreads and, most importantly, a more efficient routing process that results in better prices. The smaller the spread, the cheaper we can buy and the more expensive we can sell. The greater the spread, we would have to buy more expensive and sell cheaper, which adds an extra cost to our trades.

Symbol	Bid	Ask	!
⬇ AUDUSD.pro	0.68689	0.68691	2
⬆ EURGBP.pro	0.89397	0.89399	2
⬇ EURJPY.pro	118.945	118.947	2
⬇ EURUSD.pro	1.10401	1.10402	1
⬇ GBPJPY.pro	133.049	133.053	4
⬇ GBPUSD.pro	1.23493	1.23496	3
⬇ NZDUSD.pro	0.64242	0.64245	3
⬆ USDCAD.pro	1.31536	1.31538	2
⬇ USDCHF.pro	0.99263	0.99266	3
⬇ USDJPY.pro	107.737	107.739	2

The above table shows an example of spreads in a Pro Account. The last column, which tells us the spread, refers to spread denominated in one-tenth of a Pip. "2" would refer to "0.2 pips." We can see that the spread ranges from 0.1 Pips to 0.4 Pips depending on the Currency Pair.

Symbol	Bid	Ask	!
⬆ SPI200.fs	6637.5	6639.5	20
⬇ AUDUSD	0.68685	0.68696	11
⬆ EURGBP	0.89393	0.89404	11
⬇ EURJPY	118.940	118.952	12
⬇ EURUSD	1.10396	1.10408	12
⬇ GBPJPY	133.045	133.058	13
⬇ GBPUSD	1.23489	1.23500	11
⬇ NZDUSD	0.64238	0.64250	12
⬆ USDCAD	1.31532	1.31542	10
⬇ USDCHF	0.99258	0.99271	13
⬇ USDJPY	107.733	107.743	10

The above table shows an example of spreads in a regular account, and we can see the spreads are multiple times the size of the Pro Account. Spreads range from one Pip to 1.3 Pips

Pro Accounts usually mean you pay both the spread and a commission, and the commission varies depending on the broker and size of the trade. Commissions are usually charged per leg of the trade, meaning one for entry and for exit. The total commission for the trade once closed is what's known as the "roundtrip" commission.

As an example, a broker may charge $3.50 for one leg (either a buy or sell to enter the trade) and $3.50 for the other leg (either a buy or sell to close the trade), so the roundtrip commission is $7 (per one Standard-Lot).

Many traders want to avoid what they perceive to be paying commissions in favor of wider spreads, but this can have a large effect on the outcome of trades, especially when using greater trade size. Here are some examples:

Trading the EURUSD in a Pro Account with one Standard-Lot

- Spread of 0.1 Pip
- Traded with 1 Standard-Lot, the EURUSD Pip value = $10
- Cost of the trade in spread = $1 (0.1 x $10)
- Example of Commission cost for the trade (roundtrip) = $7
- Cost of the trade = $8

VS.

Trading the EURUSD in a regular account with one Standard-Lot

- Spread of 1.2 Pips
- Traded with one Standard-Lot, the EURUSD pip value = $10
- Cost of the trade in spread = $12 (1.2 x $10)
- No commission
- Cost of the trade = $12

If using more lots, and/or a different currency pair, then the cost of the trade would be calculated accordingly. For example:

Trading the AUDUSD in a Pro Account with four Standard-Lots

- Spread of 0.2 Pips
- Traded with one Standard-Lot, the AUDUSD Pip value = $10
- Traded with four Standard-Lots, the AUDUSD Pip value = $40
- Cost of the trade in spread = $8 (0.2 x $40)
- Example of Commission cost for the trade (roundtrip) = $28 ($7 x 4)
- Total cost of the trade = $36

VS.

Trading the AUDUSD in a regular account with four Standard-Lots

- Spread of 1.1 Pips
- Traded with one Standard-Lot, the AUDUSD Pip value = $10

- Traded with four Standard-Lots, the AUDUSD Pip value = $40
- Cost of the trade in spread = $44 (1.1 x $40)
- No commission
- Total cost of the trade = $44

Although there is no commission charged on the regular account, with larger trade sizes, the width of the spread can end up costing us more than paying commission and getting narrower spreads. The last example on the AUDUSD showed a $12 difference on the cost of the trade. With smaller trade sizes, this doesn't make as much of a difference:

Trading the AUDUSD in a Pro account with four Mini-Lots

- Spread of 0.2 Pips
- Traded with one Mini-Lot, the AUDUSD Pip value = $1
- Traded with four Mini-Lots, the AUDUSD Pip value = $4
- Cost of the trade in spread = $0.80 (0.2 x $4)
- Example of Commission cost for the trade (roundtrip) = $0.70
- Total cost of the trade = $1.50

VS.

Trading the AUDUSD in a regular account with four Mini-Lots

- Spread of 1.1 Pips
- Traded with one Mini-Lot, the AUDUSD Pip value = $1
- Traded with 4 Mini-Lots, the AUDUSD Pip value = $4
- Cost of the trade in spread = $4.40 (1.1 x $4)
- No commission
- Total cost of the trade = $4.40

The difference between the use of Standard-Lots vs Mini-Lots with the same trade example is now only $2.90 because the trade size is smaller, although the Pro Account is still favorable in terms of reduced cost. Using Micro-Lots, the cost difference is even smaller:

Trading the AUDUSD in a Pro Account with four Micro-Lots

- Spread of 0.2 Pips

- Traded with 1 Micro-Lot, the AUDUSD Pip value = $0.10
- Traded with 4 Micro-Lots, the AUDUSD Pip value = $0.40
- Cost of the trade in spread = $0.08 (0.2 x $0.40)
- Example of Commission cost for the trade (roundtrip) = $0.07
- Total cost of the trade = $0.15

VS.

Trading the AUDUSD in a regular account with four Micro-Lots

- Spread of 1.1 Pips
- Traded with 1 Micro-Lot, the AUDUSD Pip value = $0.10
- Traded with 4 Micro-Lots, the AUDUSD Pip value = $0.40
- Cost of the trade in spread = $0.44 (1.1 x $0.40)
- No commission
- Total cost of the trade = $0.44

The difference here is only $0.29 so, perhaps, it is negligible for the trader to choose one account over the other.

There is no right or wrong. It will depend on your account size – and trade size – as to what is the most cost-effective option. It is also relative to the expected profit of the trade. If you are intra-day trading, meaning the moves you are looking to catch will be smaller, then it is more advantageous to use a Pro Account and, therefore, smaller spreads, to increase profitability.

Let's say the AUDUSD example above was an intra-day trade, where the target was 15 Pips away:

- 4 Mini-Lots = $4 Pip value
- 15 Pip target x $4 Pip value = $60 expected reward
- Pro-Account Cost of trade = $1.50 (2.5% of reward)
- Regular Account Cost of trade = $4.40 (7.3% of reward)

If you are swing or position trading, then this is less important as the moves you're looking to catch will be much greater and, therefore, an extra Pip of trade cost doesn't eat so much into profit. Let's use the same example with the AUDUSD using Mini-Lots, where the target is 90 Pips away:

- 4 Mini-Lots = $4 Pip value
- 90 Pip target x $4 Pip value = $360 expected reward
- Pro-Account Cost of trade = $1.50 (0.4% of reward)
- Regular Account Cost of trade = $4.40 (1.2% of reward)

Remember the cost of the trade (spread and commission) has nothing to do with the risk of trade (what you lose if you're wrong). Whether you are right or wrong, you will still pay the spread (and commission on Pro Accounts).

Each broker is different and may charge different commissions or provide different spreads, so the above examples are not fixed for every case. We would recommend that if you have a smaller account and are day trading, then Pro Accounts make a little more sense as you will save more in cost as a percentage of your expected profits. If you are swing trading or above, then using accounts with regular spreads should be fine.

ROLLOVER AND SWAPS

When we trade Spot Forex, we trade currencies in pairs, meaning that we buy one currency and sell another at the same time. Because we're buying one of the currencies, in theory, we may want physical delivery of the currency.

For example, if we bought one standard lot of the EURUSD and we took physical delivery, UPS would knock on the door and deliver to us 100,000 EUR. As traders, we don't want physical delivery, as that would imply a few things: We would need to pay the total amount for the value of the currency we receive so we lose leverage when we take delivery; we also would then need to store a large amount of cash, which could be lost or stolen.

To avoid physical delivery of the Currency Pairs we trade, Forex brokers run a process known as "rollover," where settlement dates keep being pushed back in time.

The rollover process generates an interest rate differential between the two Currencies that make up the Pair, commonly known as the Swap

Rate or simply the "Swap." It is not imperative to understand the complexity of this process, as long as we understand that there is an interest rate differential between the two Currencies within the Currency Pair.

Each individual Currency has an interest rate set by their own central bank, so when we have two currencies together in a pair, one usually has a higher interest rate than the other. Therefore, we have an interest rate differential, which we call a "swap."

Swaps can be positive or negative, which would imply debiting or crediting interest rates payments on a regular basis. As a Forex trader, you are exposed to the differential of interest rates on a daily basis, so you either get paid or have to pay it, depending on the currencies within the pair(s) you're trading and the interest rate differential between them.

For example, you buy the EURUSD, meaning you are buying the EUR, selling the USD. Both currencies will have different interest rates that will change through time. Let's say that the interest rates are as follows:

EUR = 0.25
USD = 1.25

The differential is the difference between the two. As you are buying the EUR and selling the USD, you receive 0.25, but need to pay 1.25.

Total Swap = -1

This means that when buying the EURUSD, you will need to pay a daily amount of 1%. If it was the other way around and the euro had the higher interest rate and the dollar had the lower interest rate, then instead of paying 1%, you would receive 1%. Brokers will charge a little more on top of the swap as they are the ones doing the rollover process, so it may be that you pay 1.1% or receive 0.9%.

Most brokers would settle Swaps on a daily basis at 5 p.m. EST.

The interest rates change over time so the rollover fees (Swaps) will change too. You can see the live rollover rates on your trading platform; they often show as "roll B" and "roll S", or "swap long" and "swap short", which tells you the amount when you buy versus the amount when you sell:

The Swaps are either collected or charged regardless of whether you win or lose. If you win a trade and there are negative swaps incurred, then you will make your profit, minus the rollover fee (Swap). If you win a trade and there are positive Swaps incurred, then you will make your profit, plus the rollover fee. The same is true if you lose: The Swap is added or subtracted to your closed position, depending on whether you collected or paid the Swap.

Swaps can be used to gain interest on your positions, which is often used for longer-term position trades or investments.

Example:

- Short EURUSD 1 Standard-Lot
- Swap is collected at $4.68 per day
- Trade lasts one year (365 days), continuing in the direction of your trade
- Total Swaps collected = $1,708.2 ($4.68 x 365)

The rate of return on swaps depends on the size of the account. Let's say that this trader was using a leverage account of 50:1. (50:1 is the maximum limit for leverage on spot Forex in the United States, as set by US law.)

- 1 Standard Lot of shorting EURUSD = $100,000
- Required margin to enter the trade = $2,000
- Swaps collected = $1,708.20
- Rate of return = 85.41%

If you were right on the trade, you would also collect your profit. If you were wrong on the trade and it took a year to stop out, you would take your loss but collect the Swap of $1,708.20. If price didn't move very much in a year so you didn't hit your stop or target, then you're still in the trade – and you've still collected the swap of $1,708.20

As said before, the rollover process normally happens at 5 p.m. EST every day, so if you are day trading and are out of your positions before 5 p.m., then you will neither pay nor collect Swaps.

It's important to be aware of the Swaps and rollover fees if you do plan on holding trades for multiple days, weeks, months or years. The longer you hold onto the trade, the more you will either pay or receive on Swaps, which can either increase or decrease the total profit/loss in your account.

The rollover fees should not deter you from entering a high-probability trade, nor encourage you to enter a low-probability trade for the sake of the Swap. Being profitable on your trade and then paying a small amount of rollover fees is better than losing your trade and gaining a small amount of rollover.

For longer-term positions where you aim to capitalize on longer expo-sure to collecting Swaps, you still will want to enter the position where you have AutoClimate™ and AutoUFOs® in your favor.

Spot Forex Benefits

According to investopedia.com, "A Spot Forex trade, also known as a spot transaction, refers to the purchase or sale of a foreign currency, financial instrument or commodity for instant delivery on a specified spot date."

Pros	Cons
Leverage (often depending on regulation)	Decentralized (No Exchange)
Interest Rates (could be positive)	Interest Rates (could be negative)
Extremely Liquid	Pip Values vary
Trading is open 24 hours during weekdays	
Diverse combination of FX Pairs	

Common Applications	Direction
All Styles of Trading	Long and Short

Every single financial market that is available to trade has pros and cons, and all have their place. Forex is an interesting instrument to trade because it can be used for all styles of trading; from day trading to investing and in both directions (up and down).

The Swap exposure is something that is unique to Spot Forex. Traders can trade currencies through other derivative markets, such as futures, and can capitalize on the movements of the currencies, but they would not be exposed to Swaps and, therefore, would not have the opportu-nity to collect extra interest on their trades.

The high liquidity and diverse combinations of FX pairs also provide many opportunities to traders, whatever style of trader they are.

Example of a Spot Forex trade:

In this example, we are looking at a NZDUSD trade, using AutoUFOs®
on the 8-minute chart to go long. The style of trading is intra-day trading
as the entry timeframe is relatively small. If we are looking to go long
on this timeframe, this would mean that a higher timeframe (probably a
60-minute chart) has a confirmed upwards climate, which we would see
as a thick blue dot on the AutoClimate™ app.

Here are the parameters of the trade:

Entry Price: 0.6415
Stop Loss: 0.6410
Target Price: 0.6435
Trade Size: 8 MINI-Lots
Pip Value: $1/Pip x 8 = $8/Pip
Trade Risk: $40 (five Pips)

Notional Value: NZD80k ≈ $51,320
Margin Required: NZD800 ≈ $513.20
Leverage: 100:1

AutoClimate™ is providing us with our direction (long) and AutoUFOs® are providing our Entry, Stop and Target prices. In this example, the total risk of the trade is $40, which is made up of the 5-Pip difference between entry and stop, a Pip value of $1 and 8 mini-lots:

5 Pips x $1/Pip x 8 mini-lots = $40

(5 x 8 x 1 = $40)

1 Mini-Lot of buying NZDUSD is equal to 10,000 NZD, so 8 Mini-Lots means the trade is worth 80,000 NZD (at the time of writing, worth roughly $51,320 USD).

With a leverage of 100:1 (which would not be available within the US, but in other countries), then the total amount required in the account to place the trade is one-one-hundredth of the notional value:

$51,320 / 100 = $513.20

The result of the trade was the following:

Price went up and hit the target, meaning the profit was realized. End result:

Profit: $160 (20 Pips)

Reward to risk: 4:1

Return on Investment: 31.17% ($160/$513.20)

The return on investment refers to the amount of money made versus the amount of money needed in the account to place the trade.

TRADING TIMEFRAMES

The Timeframes used when trading, are very much linked to trading styles. The longer-term the trading style, the bigger the timeframes used.

Whatever the style of trading, multiple timeframes are to be used when planning trades so that we can look at the trade from multiple angles and increase probability. Each timeframe seeks to uncover different types of market information, which, when combined, would confirm if a trading opportunity is available or not. If you were to only look at one timeframe, you may end up with an okay trade, but be unaware of information in another timeframe that would actually invalidate your trade.

As we referenced before, this is similar to a doctor taking X-rays of a broken bone from multiple angles, to better understand what is going on and take more appropriate action. We want to do the same with our trading.

However, we don't want to use too many timeframes because it can become over-complicated with too much conflicting information, which makes it hard to be decisive. Like everything, it's about balance: we don't want to be too complicated or too simple.

We will use two to three timeframes to plan a trade:

- COMMON timeframe
- EDGE timeframe
- REACTIVE timeframe

Normally, we would suggest using only the COMMON and EDGE timeframes. The REACTIVE timeframe is usually only used by conservative traders who want to add additional layers to their analysis before placing their trades.

COMMON TIMEFRAME

Thought: The only way to make money is to have more people buy after we buy or sell after we sell.

Definition: Classical time intervals available in all trading platforms. These are the timeframes used by everyone:

15-min / 60-min / 4-hour / Daily / Weekly & Monthly

Aim: This timeframe is used to identify the current Market Environment (climate) to help decide which direction to trade (being a buyer or being a seller). This timeframe can also be used to identify setups where great quantities of new buyers or sellers may be motivated to enter the market after us.

If others buy after you buy, then they help to push price up and closer to your target. If others sell after you sell, then they help to push price down and closer to your target as well. If you were the last person buying or selling, then you would see the market turn against you. For the market to continue moving in your direction, you need more people to buy after you buy or sell after you sell.

This is why we use a COMMON timeframe, so we can identify when a market is not only appealing to us, but appealing to others, in order to drive people to act after we act. To see what many others are seeing, we need to look at the same timeframes that they are using. This implies using time intervals that are available in all trading platforms and, therefore, visible and likely to be used by many other traders.

The following timeframes are the most commonly used: 15-min, 60-min, 4-hour, Daily, Weekly & Monthly. They are available on every platform in the world. Therefore, these are the timeframes we use for our Common timeframe analysis.

We use this timeframe to decide whether to be long or short or to not trade at all (Question No. 1 that we should always ask ourselves when we trade). Question No. 1 is answered by AutoClimate™, so we use AutoClimate™ on our Common timeframe.

Of course, AutoClimate™, as an app, can be applied to any timeframe. It will do its job and analyze market data, giving us probabilities associated with upwards or downwards climates on any timeframe we apply it to. However, it makes more sense to apply it solely to our Common timeframe – where most other traders are looking and making buying or selling decisions – to answer our Question No. 1.

The Common timeframe is the highest timeframe we use in our analysis and, usually, the higher the timeframe, the more buying or selling power. Therefore, we will also use our Common timeframe to identify where greater quantities of buyers or sellers may be motivated to enter the market after we enter and, therefore, increase probability that our trades reach our targets.

EDGE TIMEFRAME

Thought: Entering a market should be as invisible as possible since we need sellers to buy from and buyers to sell to.

Definition: Unique time-intervals used by large market players' computerized trading systems (often Fibonacci numbers):

2, 8, 21, 55, 144, 377, etc. min / ticks / volume
(Lower than COMMON timeframe)

Aim: This timeframe is used to identify where Un-Filled Orders (UFOs) are available. We are looking for UFOs that belong to large market players – more specifically, the ones injected by their computerized trading systems.

Although we want to use Common (often-used and visible) timeframes to direct our choice of long, short, or no-trade, we need to use a less visible timeframe to enter our trades. We need others to buy after we buy and sell after we sell and we need others to sell to us when we want to buy and buy from us when we want to sell. If you were to try and buy at the same price at which everybody else is trying to buy, you may not get filled as the sellers at that price are selling to the other buyers who were there before you. This could result in missing a trade or you may end up having to buy at a more expensive price. The same is true if you want to sell: if you try to sell at the same price at which everybody else is trying to sell, you would risk not being filled.

When we enter the market, we want to enter as invisibly as possible, using timeframes that are not used by the masses but are instead used by large market players' computerized systems. If we enter on rarely used timeframes, where large market players enter the markets, it is more likely that retail traders are buying from us and selling to us. The market then moves in our direction and the retail traders use their common timeframes to buy after we buy and sell after we sell.

To identify the UFOs that large market players are placing on the timeframes used by their computerized systems, we need to understand what timeframes those are likely to be. The following timeframes are often used by these systems: 2, 8, 21, 55, 144, 377, etc., on minute-charts as well as tick (activity) and volume (shares) charts.

You may notice that these numbers are in the Fibonacci sequence. Fibonacci numbers are commonly used in computing and in the large market players' computerized trading systems.

It is not imperative that you use Fibonacci timeframes; the AutoUFOs® will work on other timeframes too. However, there is a higher probability of finding the orders of large market players if we use the same timeframes they do.

Not all platforms will allow you to see "odd" timeframes; it may depend on your subscription level. For example, TradingView only allows it with a subscription level of Pro or higher.

Ideally, we want to enter invisibly with large market players and away from the attention of retail traders, in a larger-context environment where many traders are likely to enter after we enter. This is why the Common timeframe used will be higher than the Edge timeframe used.

This is combining direct forces and indirect forces: entering with the direct forces of high quantities of buy or sell orders, aided by the indirect forces of climate on a higher timeframe, which would encourage others to add buy or sell orders in our favor.

We combine the indirect forces on the Common timeframe with a corresponding Edge timeframe (direct forces). The Edge timeframe will always be lower than the common timeframe as it's used for entry, which is something that we need to be more specific on, keeping our risk as low as possible.

The following table shows the Common timeframes used and their corresponding Edge timeframes, both for custom timeframes (available on Pro Accounts on TradingView) and for standard timeframes that are available on all trading platforms:

CUSTOMIZED

common		edge
60 min	→	8 min
240 min	→	21 min
Daily	→	55 min
Weekly	→	144 min
Monthly	→	377 min
common		edge

These timeframes are combined as follows:

- 60-minute > 8-minute
- 240-minute > 21-minute
- Daily > 55-minute
- Weekly > 144-minute
- Monthly > 377-minute

STANDARD

common		edge

common		edge
60 min	→	5 min
240 min	→	15 min
Daily	→	60 min
Weekly	→	240 min
Monthly	→	Daily

common		edge

In the case of the standard set of timeframes, we use the closest commonly available timeframe to the customized set as is possible (for the Edge timeframe):

- 60-minute > 5-minute
- 240-minute > 15-minute
- Daily > 60-minute
- Weekly > 240-minute
- Monthly > Daily

REACTIVE TIMEFRAME

This timeframe is optional and is usually only used by conservative traders looking for additional evidence.

Thought: It is unlikely that UFOs are cancelled as long as we trade in the right side of the market (climate), unless the Market Climate was to suddenly change

Definition: Unique time-intervals used by large market players' computerized trading systems (often Fibonacci numbers):

3, 8, 21, 55, 144, 377, etc. min / ticks / volume
(Lower than Edge timeframe)

Aim: This optional timeframe is used to confirm that UFOs are found where UFOs were expected to be (based on the Edge timeframe).

For example:

COMMON Timeframe = Daily, blue thick dot on AutoClimate™ (confirmed upwards climate, look for long opportunities on edge timeframe)

EDGE Timeframe = 55-minute, green UFO lining up as a good opportunity

Rather than simply place this trade, some conservative traders may choose to wait until price comes into their original entry UFO and go down a timeframe (21-minute) to get confirmation of a long position by seeing buy UFOs form on this timeframe around the same price points.

The presence of a UFO on the smaller timeframe within the UFO on the edge timeframe gives you more evidence that the place on the chart where you expected UFOs does indeed have UFOs.

Let's say you have an entry UFO to buy on the Edge timeframe and the numbers are: 1.1500 - 1.1400. If on the reactive timeframe, as price comes into the original UFO, you see a green (buy) UFO form at 1.1490 - 1.1465, you now have a small buy UFO within a bigger buy UFO. This adds to the probabilities of price going up, because there are now two different stacks of buy orders within one another.

This is a more conservative approach as it requires an additional step in the process to increase probabilities. The downside is that it requires you to act manually. You will need to wait until orders form on the Reactive timeframe and enter the trade at that point, which means needing to be able to execute quicker and be more available to access your platforms/brokers.

It could also mean that you, unfortunately, miss out on some trades due to the nature of needing to execute manually. It could be that you can't place the order in time or you're not available to monitor it at the time price enters the edge UFO. Sometimes, price will enter the edge timeframe UFO and take off without forming new UFOs on the reactive timeframe, which would also lead to missing trades.

The reactive timeframe is not one that is needed but it will not necessarily hurt to use it if you'd like some more evidence and probabilities on your side for your trades. The higher the probability, the fewer losses you would take.

Once again, we will use Fibonacci timeframes, so that we are looking at the same charts that large market players' orders are executed on, and they correspond with the Edge and Common timeframes used:

CUSTOMIZED

common		edge	reactive
60 min	→	8 min	3 min
240 min	→	21 min	8 min
Daily	→	55 min	21 min
Weekly	→	144 min	55 min
Monthly	→	377 min	144 min
common		edge	reactive

STANDARD

common		edge	reactive
60 min	→	5 min	1 min
240 min	→	15 min	3 min
Daily	→	60 min	15 min
Weekly	→	240 min	60 min
Monthly	→	Daily	240 min
common		edge	reactive

TIMEFRAMES PER STYLE

Depending on the style of trader you are and how long you want your trades to last for, you will use different combinations of timeframes.

The longer-term the style, the higher timeframes used:

CUSTOMIZED

	common		edge	reactive
Intraday	60 min	→	8 min	3 min
Swing	240 min	→	21 min	8 min
Position	Daily	→	55 min	21 min
	Weekly	→	144 min	55 min
Investor	Monthly	→	377 min	144 min

common		edge	reactive

STANDARD

	common		edge	reactive
Intraday	60 min	→	5 min	1 min
Swing	240 min	→	15 min	3 min
Position	Daily	→	60 min	15 min
	Weekly	→	240 min	60 min
Investor	Monthly	→	Daily	240 min

common		edge	reactive

Depending on how active you want to be within the styles of trading, there are often choices available to you. The lower the timeframes, the more frequent the trades, meaning the more active you would need to be. The higher the timeframes, the less frequent the trades, so you would need to be more passive.

If you want to be an intra-day trader, here are two options:

- Using the 60-minute in combination with the 8-minute chart (or 5-minute) is used solely for intra-day trading, as the trades will form, trigger and close more than likely within one day.
- 240 minutes combined with 21 minutes can be used for intra-day and swing trading, as the duration of trades is likely to be hours, although it could run into a day or two. It could be seen as short-term swing or longer-term day trading.

As a swing trader, your choices could be:

- 240 minutes combined with 21 minutes (this would be shorter-term swing trading)
- Daily combined with 55 minutes (this will take slightly longer for the trades to play out)

As a position trader, valid choices could be:

- Daily with 55 minutes (it would be used as shorter-term position trading)
- Weekly with 144 minutes (which will take slightly longer than the prior example for trades to play out)

As an investor, a smart approach could be using the Monthly chart combined with the 377-minute (or Daily), as the trades will take weeks to months to form, trigger and close.

TRADING METHODOLOGY: Overview

A key goal in trading is to produce consistent results. This can only be done if a repetitive mechanical process is in place, as this would produce consistent action leading to the desired consistent results. Many traders practice a variety of methodologies, going through a process of trial and error, often knee-jerking to their experiences. This is a normal and very human thing to do; however, it will almost certainly end up with inconsistent results as the action is inconsistent.

The only way to obtain consistent results with inconsistent action would be to have lots of luck on our side, which is obviously not a serious proposal. Luck cannot last forever and, although it may occasionally produce big gains, the same action will often result in big losses. If we play with luck in our financial lives, it could be good or it could be bad. We have no way of knowing or predicting which one it will be and we will end up riding the rollercoaster, watching our trading accounts go up and down, without understanding why. Most traders end up giving up for this reason, deeming trading to be "risky" or "gambling."

In reality, trading is no different than any other business. If we knew nothing about a particular industry, yet we opened a business in it and randomly tried various business strategies for no more than a few days, while trialing other things at the same time, changing direction often without tracking results, we would expect failure. If success was reached, we would understand it to be luck.

In any business, the structure of a plan that tells them what to do and how to do it, is key. Just like an industrial process that aims for quality, an ideal way on how to understand and use a Trading Methodology is to represent it as a flowchart:

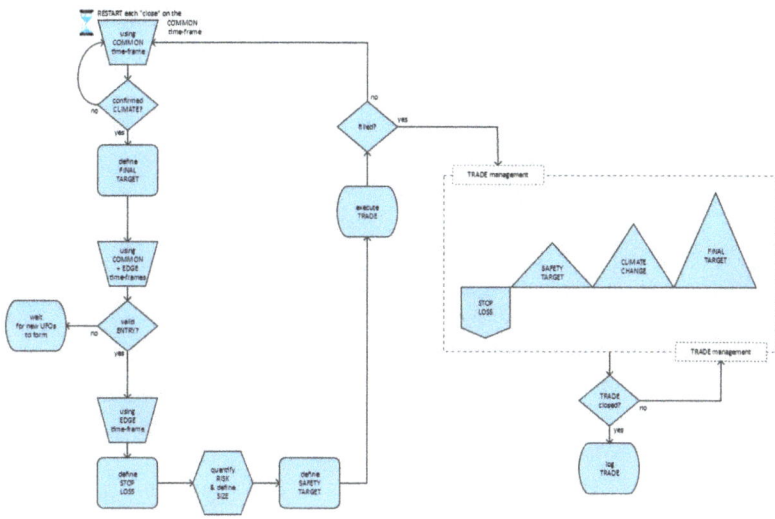

By using something like this, it is easier for us to behave mechanically, by looking at, and acting on, one box at a time in sequence. If at any point while going through the flowchart we are analyzing a trading opportunity and it does not meet the criteria for the box we're looking at, we do not take the trade.

In the same way, an industrial process to make something requires a step-by-step approach; if one of the steps cannot be fulfilled, or malfunctions, the manufacturer would not continue making that particular product.

Let's break the flowchart into pieces:

- It will help to understand each of its components
- It will also outline the step-by-step approach to trading
- It will define the specific rules to follow with discipline

Please keep in mind that throughout the following section, we will be using two main Currency Pair examples to illustrate how the methodology would work: the GBPAUD (long) and the EURUSD (short).

Although we've used these two pairs to illustrate the application of the strategy, the methodology applies to every other Currency Pair as well.

Please notice that in the "Risk and Size" section, we will also use a EURCAD Currency Pair example to reinforce how size is calculated.

TRADING METHODOLOGY: Climate

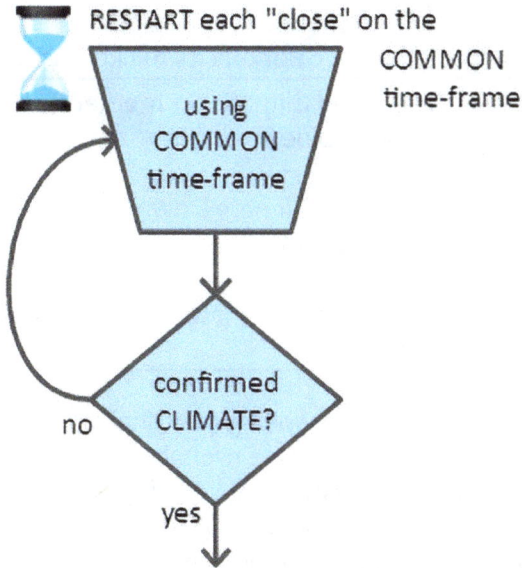

This step is first on the flowchart because it answers Question No. 1 for us: "Should I be a buyer, seller, or not trade at all?" If the climate were undefined, we would simply stop here and not move on to analyze that market further. Instead, we would either wait for a new candle to form and re-analyze market climate, or move on and analyze another Currency Pair.

Timeframe	COMMON
Tools	AutoClimate™ app
Aim	This step consists of assessing the Market Climate (current Market Environment) to decide in which direction to trade (Long or Short) or to avoid trading at this time
Action	Apply AutoClimate™ in the Common timeframe and check the dot color and its thickness
Possible Outcomes	• Confirmed Climate Up-Market: Thick dot + Sapphire blue color • Confirmed Climate Down-Market: Thick dot + Ruby red color • Unconfirmed Climate: Thin dot (no matter the color)

This step is used to determine whether we analyze an opportunity further as we want to know if we have probabilities enough to either the upside or the downside to justify even placing a trade. Similarly, if the climate were to change after placing your trade – for example, from confirmed up-climate to an unconfirmed climate – then you would cancel the trade. This would be because the answer to Question No. 1 would have changed and, therefore, invalidated the trade.

Whichever timeframe you use for your Common timeframe, this will be the one you use for analyzing Climate. This implies rechecking the market at the close of each candle to re-analyze Climate and to check that your trade or trades are still valid, or alter them if the Climate has changed.

For example, if you use the four-hour timeframe for your Common timeframe, you will need to re-analyze your trade and check the Climate after the close of that four-hour candle. If you are intra-day trading on a smaller timeframe and you use the one-hour chart for your Common timeframe, then you will need to re-analyze at the end of the one-hour candle.

This is directly affected by how busy you are, your availability of time and your trading style. If you have time during the day and can check your trades frequently, then you would be able to enact the methodology using a smaller timeframe for your Common timeframe.

You may be someone who doesn't have time during the day to check your trades regularly. You may be working all day without access to your trading account; perhaps you are a pilot flying for multiple hours on long-distance flights where you're totally disconnected from the internet. If this is the case, then your trading style should not be based on using one-hour or four-hour timeframes for your Common timeframe because you will not be able to check your trades as often as you need to in order to enact your trading methodology consistently.

Perhaps in this case, you would use a daily chart or a weekly chart and, therefore, be a swing or position trader. If you still want to day trade and use the smaller timeframes, you would need to be strict about cancelling all of your trades that don't fill in the time that you are able to monitor them.

Let's say you have two hours to sit and trade before your flight. You could place your trades in that time, following the rules strictly and re-checking after the close of the one-hour timeframe. Once the two hours are up, all trades are cancelled or closed. This may cut off some profits for trades that are already open by taking profits earlier, but it may also limit some losses from trades that are already open.

Regardless of your trading style (which first and foremost must fit with your lifestyle), every time there is a close on the common timeframe, you need to go back and revisit the plan to see whether or not your trades have been invalidated and you need to cancel them, or to confirm that they can remain in play until the end of the next close.

Climate examples

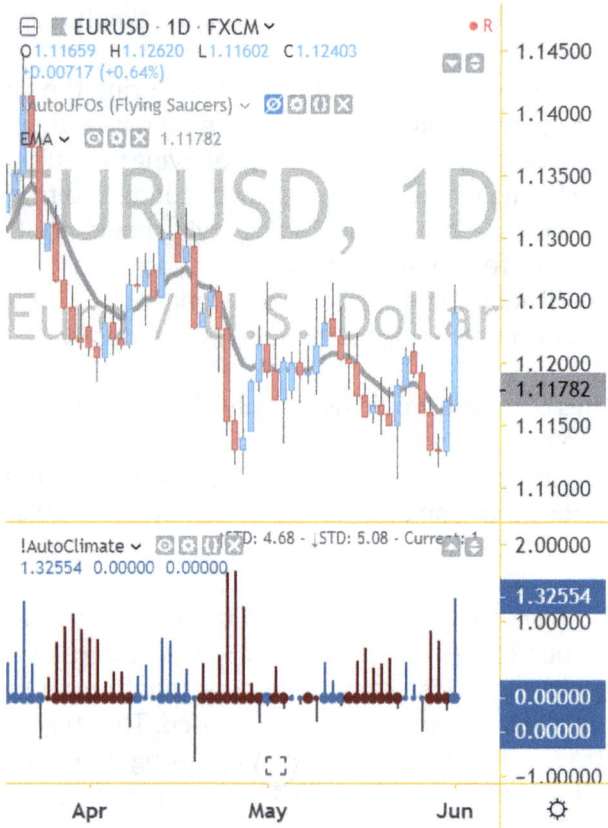

Confirmed upward climate:

Thick blue dot showing on the AutoClimate™ app, depicting that we have an upwards market environment with probabilities to the upside. This gives us permission to continue with the flowchart, analyzing long opportunities.

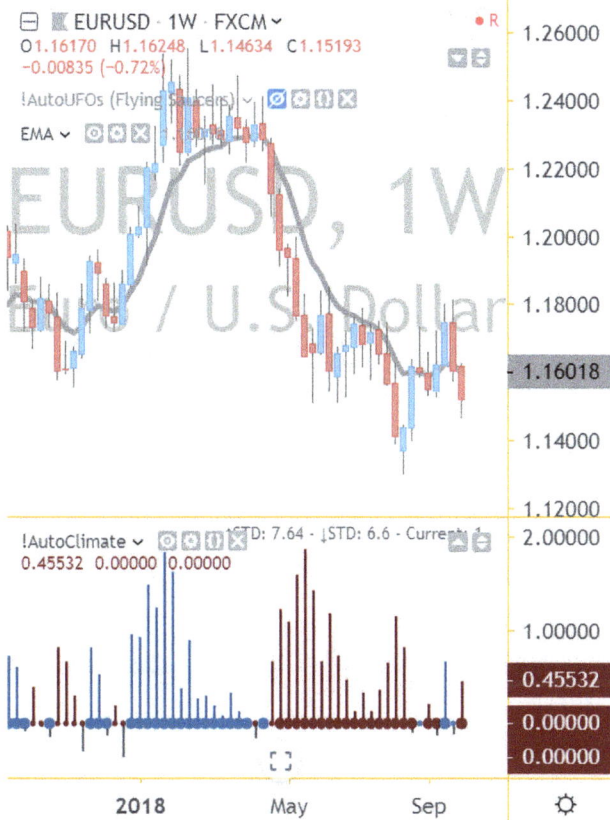

Confirmed downward climate:

Thick red dot showing on the AutoClimate™ app, depicting that we have a downwards market environment with probabilities to the downside. This gives us permission to continue with the flowchart, analyzing short opportunities.

Unconfirmed climates:

Thin dot of either color, depicting lack of probabilities either long or short, so therefore we do nothing, analyze another market or wait for a new candle on the Common timeframe.

As we mentioned before, there are other things we need to do when we analyze climate. We want to ensure that we have sustainability on our side and that price isn't too far away from an ideal trading price (the EMA value on the Common timeframe).

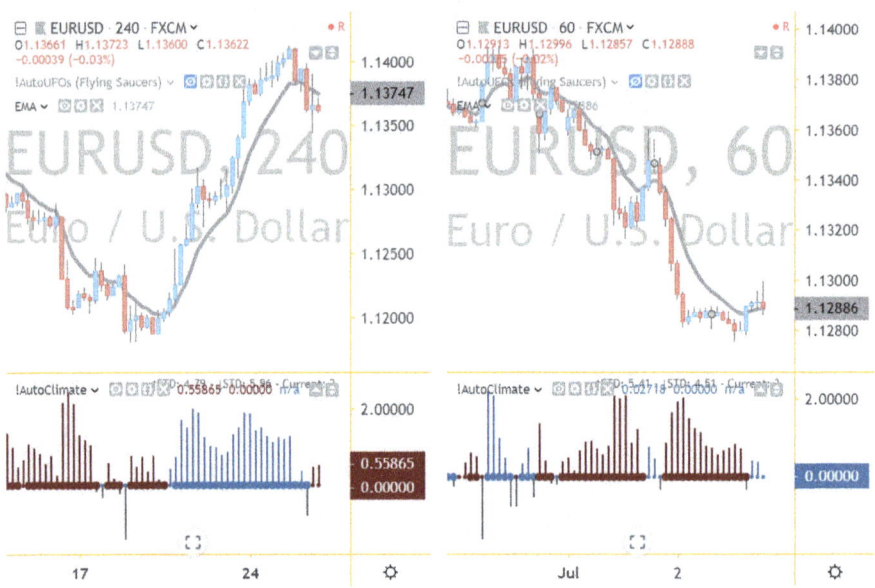

Sustainability

We look at the sustainability stats to determine if we still have probabilities for a continuous move in the given direction. If so, we are happy to continue with our analysis. If not, we either invalidate the trade or we go ahead but only use half of our normal position size, to guard against the lower probabilities.

Let's say we look at a market and the sustainability stats suggest that the EURUSD usually goes down for seven candles on a four-hour chart and the market is currently on its sixth candle to the downside. This means we still have four hours to get into the trade and it still have sustainability probabilities. Remember, the entry is taken on a much smaller timeframe (our Edge timeframe). Therefore, we may be looking for an entry on a 21-minute chart and have four hours left for the trade to be valid.

If the EURUSD usually goes down for seven candles on a four-hour chart and we are on candle number eight to the downside, then we have already surpassed sustainability probabilities. Therefore, if we were to execute a trade, we could decide to do so at half the usual position size.

ATR

If the ATR spread is particularly wide (meaning the line coming out of the AutoClimate™ dot is long), we may choose not to continue with the flowchart in favor of prioritizing our time with trades that are more likely to hit our entries sooner. The ATR spread tells us how far price is away from our ideal trading price, which is the 9-EMA on the common timeframe. Since our entries need to be based on UFOs that envelop the Common 9-EMA, we ideally want to focus on trades that are going to be closer to that price as they will trigger sooner and be more likely to stay valid before triggered.

TERMINOLOGY CORNER

Rival UFO

Existing Un-Filled Orders (UFOs) which are contrary to the Trade direction (normally used as Exit Prices). For example, if you are looking to go long (buy), then rival UFOs would be sell (red) UFOs. If you are looking to go short (sell), then the rival UFOs would be buy (green) UFOs. They are often used for targets as they highlight areas where price may turn so we would want to take profit before price is likely to turn against us.

Ally UFO

Existing UFOs representing Un-Filled Orders which are compatible with the Trade direction (normally used as Entry Prices), or new UFOs formed as the Market moved in the expected desired direction after entering a trade (normally used to trail stops and lock on profits).

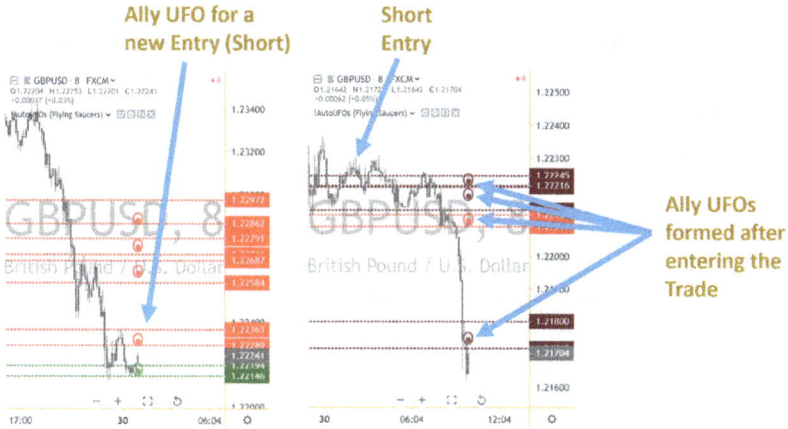

In the image above, the trader would have gone short originally, and then new red (sell) UFOs formed as price moved down (in favor of a short position). These would be ally UFOs because they helped the trade move in the desired direction.

If the trader went long, then the appearance of new green (buy) UFOs would be ally UFOs, as they would help to push price upwards, which would be the desired trade direction.

Using these types of UFOs to trail a stop allows us to lock in profits using areas on the chart where there are likely to be orders, objectively highlighted by the technology. Remember, UFOs represent areas on a price chart where there is likely to be an imbalance of orders, either buy orders or sell orders. If new UFOs form that align with your trade direction, then new orders are being added to the market, helping to push price further into profit for you. If UFOs are normally used to help us calculate our entries and stops, but we're already in a trade, we can trail our stop behind these new UFOs.

This way, if the market climate changes or price unexpectedly moves against us, although we wouldn't have hit our target, we would be stopped out at some level of profit. Instead of moving the stop to the middle of nowhere, based on arbitrary parameters, we only trail the stop behind objective evidence that new orders are present.

As long as you are trading with the climate, then as new UFOs form, if price returns to them, it will usually react and continue in the direction of the existing climate. If price continues to move against the UFO and breaks it, then it is likely to signal a change of climate, meaning we would want to be out anyway. This is why we would use ally UFOs to trail our stops.

An easy way to summarize rival and ally UFOs is to think "is that UFO likely to do what I want or the opposite of what I want?" If you're long, buy UFOs are allies and sell UFOs are rivals. If you're short, buy UFOs are rivals so sell UFOs are allies.

TRADING METHODOLOGY:
Define Final Target

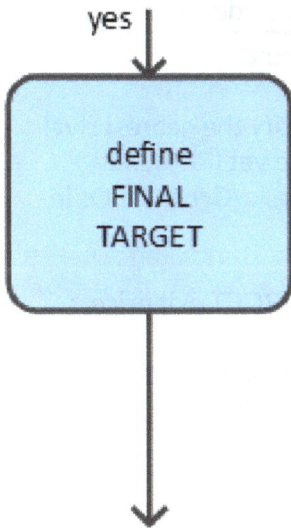

yes

define
FINAL
TARGET

This is the second step of the methodology after determining that you have a confirmed and sustainable climate. This step comes at this point, even though we have yet to find an entry, because it uses the same timeframe as the climate step. This saves you time switching between timeframes back and forth as you go through your trading process, but most importantly it also saves you time going through an entire process before realizing that you don't have enough profit potential on your trade.

We will be using UFOs to identify targets, so if you have a target (rival) UFO that is very close to your ideal entry price (9-EMA), then your profit margin is very limited. This would make the rest of the process irrelevant so we can save our time analyzing this trade and move on to another opportunity. If the target UFO is far away, then you have room to make more profit, which means going to the next step and continuing with the process is more likely to be worth it.

This comes back to having balance in our trades; probability, risk and reward. If we take trades where our targets are very close, this may mean we end up risking $10 to make $5, or $10 to make $2, or $10 to make $8, etc. If we take a lot of those types of trades and get stopped out a few times, we need to be right a lot more often to balance out the losses. Ideally, we want to take trades that have higher rewards available, so we may risk $10 to make $20, or $10 to make $30, or $10 to make $50. This way we can be right a reasonable amount of the time but we don't have to be right that frequently to make, at least, a small profit over time. Our losses are smaller than our gains and that makes for a more consistent approach to our trading.

Timeframe	COMMON
Tools	AutoUFOs® app
Aim	This step consists of identifying the price location at which to exit and conclude the trade for a profit
Action	Stay with the Common timeframe Turn on AutoUFOs® and identify the nearest rival UFO that has not been reached yet (Ruby/Red UFOs in Up-Markets and Emerald/Green UFOs in Down-Markets) Use that price as the FINAL TARGET exit price Add 2 Pips to the Target Price when planning on a Short Trade (Buy Order is your Target)
Possible Outcomes	• Rival UFO very close: Low Reward-to-Risk Ratio, discard the trade • Rival UFO far away: Use that price to be set as the FINAL TARGET (use the number closest to current price) • Current price is already inside of a Rival UFO: Use the next UFO • No rival UFO available as the Market is making new all-time highs or lows: NO TARGET, instead trail stop as new ally UFOs form

We are using the UFOs on the common timeframe to help us confirm if the opportunity is worth analyzing further, based on if we have room to make decent profits. If the closest rival UFOs are close to ideal entry price, we discard the trade. If the UFOs are further away, we use the numbers provided to us by the UFOs as our Final Target. UFOs provide two price numbers, as they show us the range of orders. For our final target price, we will use the number that is closest to current price, meaning the lower number on the red (sell) UFO and the higher number on the green (buy) UFO.

If we are using the buy (green) UFO as our Final Target, then we need to add two pips to the reference price provided by AutoUFOs®. The reason for this comes back to the difference between the Bid and the Ask. Usually, Forex brokers and platforms plot the Bid on their charts so the chart you are looking at is a reflection of the Bid price.

We sell to the Bid so using the Bid numbers for our sell orders is not a problem as it would be accurate. However, we buy from the Ask, which is not the price plotted on the chart. To counteract this, we will need to buy slightly higher than what the chart shows us. This is true for Final Targets, entries and stops. Every buy order we have, we need to add a couple of Pips to the reference numbers. If we didn't add a couple of Pips, we risk missing our fills, meaning that we could miss entries on good trades, or only just miss hitting our targets, or get stopped out by a Pip, only to see it turn in our direction.

We need to always add two Pips to every buy order, which means, when identifying our Final Targets, if our target is a green UFO, we add two Pips to the higher number given by the AutoUFOs®.

If current price is within the closest rival UFO, we ignore that UFO and use the next one. Let's say you are long, so you are looking for red (sell) UFOs for your final target. The closest one is at 1.1150 and the next one up is at 1.1298. If price is already within the 1.1150 UFO, you will take the next one up at 1.1298.

If you are short, you are therefore looking for green (buy) UFOs for your Final Target. Let's say the closest one is at 0.9856 and the next closest one is at 0.9675. If price is within the 0.9856 UFO, then discard it and choose the 0.9675 UFO as your final target.

We use UFOs for our targets so that we can take our profits and get out of our trades before a possibility of price turning against us. However, in an upwards climate, sell orders tend to be canceled (not always, but it is reasonably common). Equally, in a downwards climate, buy orders tend to be canceled. If price is already within a rival UFO ,that is going against the climate, then some of those orders are already filled, making the set of orders even less likely to cause a turn in the markets. This is why we would discard these kinds of rival UFOs and instead choose the next closest rival UFO as our reference for our Final Target.

If there are no rival UFOs, which usually means price is at an all-time high or an all-time low, then we have no reference given to us by the objective analysis of AutoUFOs®. The only option available to us is to trail our stop, and lock in profits as we go. This means placing the trade with no Final Target and, instead, managing the trade once it has already triggered, trailing our stop behind price based on ally UFOs. This is the only scenario where we do not predetermine our Final Target and execute our trade with it already planned.

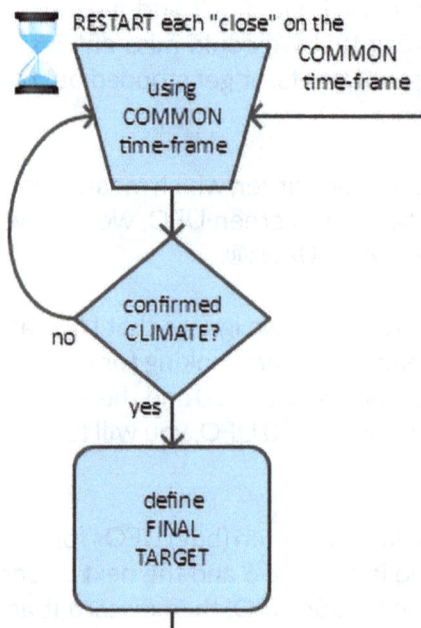

We analyze first the Climate, giving us our validity, and then trade direction, if we have a confirmed and sustainable climate.

Once we know whether we're going long or short, we can then know which are our rival UFOs and which are our ally UFOs. This then directs us to find our Final Target on the same common timeframe, taking the closest rival UFO (that price isn't already in) as the reference price for our target. We use the closest number to current price as the Final Target price (lower number on red UFOs, higher number on green UFOs).

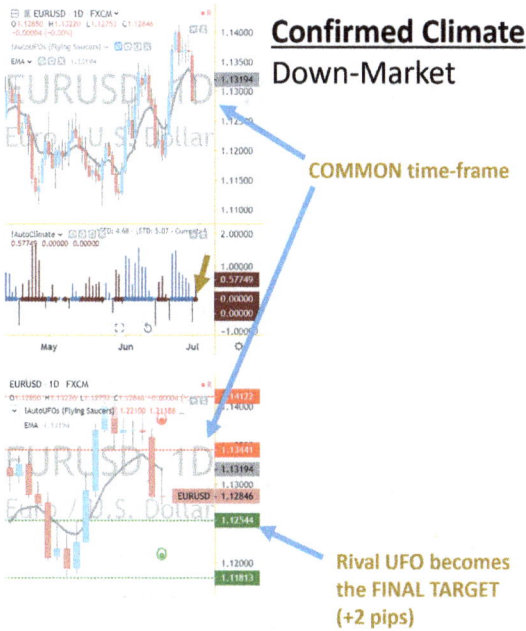

Confirmed Climate
Down-Market

COMMON time-frame

Rival UFO becomes
the FINAL TARGET
(+2 pips)

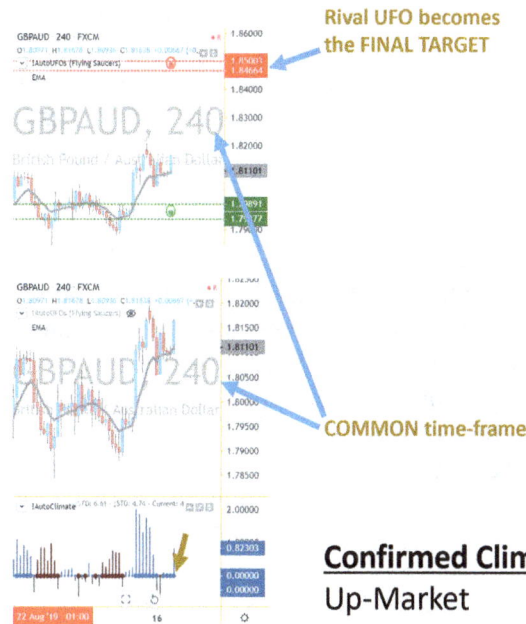

Rival UFO becomes
the FINAL TARGET

COMMON time-frame

Confirmed Climate
Up-Market

TRADING METHODOLOGY: Entry

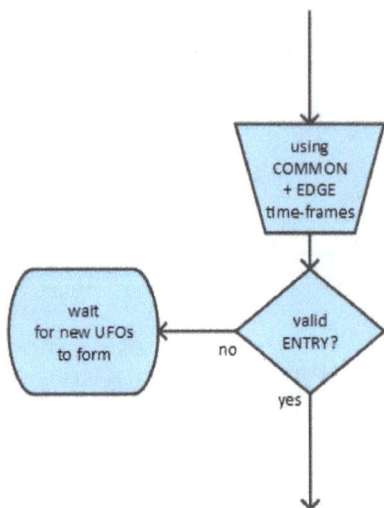

```
                    │
                    ▼
            ┌───────────────┐
             \    using     /
              \  COMMON    /
               \  + EDGE  /
                \time-frames/
                 └────┬────┘
                      ▼
 ┌──────────┐      ◇
 │   wait   │    ◇   ◇
 │for new UFOs│◄─◇ valid ◇
 │  to form  │ no◇ ENTRY?◇
 └──────────┘    ◇   ◇
                   ◇
                  yes
                   │
                   ▼
```

The next step, once the climate and the final target are defined, is to identify the entry to our potential trade setup. This requires combining both the Common and the Edge timeframes.

The tools we use are specifically designed to combine direct and indirect forces, which, as we already know, increases the probability of the trade's success. We use the Common timeframe for the indirect forces, as it's a bigger timeframe and we want more people to buy after we buy or sell after we sell. We use the Edge timeframe for our direct forces, ideally on the Fibonacci timeframes, to enter as invisibly as possible, but with large market players' buy and sell orders (which is the most direct force there is in the market: buy orders and sell orders).

If the entry is valid, meaning the indirect force on the Common timeframe and the direct force on the Edge timeframe line up with each other, then we continue with our process and further analyze our trade opportunity. If the entry is not valid, we may have to wait for new UFOs to form, which may give us a valid setup for an entry on a trade. If new UFOs don't form in the right areas, we go back to the start of the flowchart on a different Currency Pair.

Timeframe	COMMON + EDGE
Tools	AutoUFOs® app (Edge timeframe) + 9-period EMA (Common timeframe)
Aim	This step consists of identifying ally UFOs in the Edge timeframe with values that are similar to and around the EMA value found in the Common timeframe
Action	Stay with the Common timeframe, turn on the 9-EMA (9-period Exponential Moving Average) and make a note of its current value Switch to the Edge timeframe, turn on AutoUFOs® and identify the nearest ally UFO that envelops the current EMA found in the Common timeframe Add two Pips to the Entry Price when planning on a Long Trade (Buy Order)
Possible Outcomes	• There are no ally UFOs: Wait for new UFOs to form • There are ally UFOs but they are not aligned with the EMA: Wait for new UFOs to form in the right location • There is only one ally UFO perfectly aligned with the EMA = Entry • There are multiple ally UFOs overlapping each other where one of them is aligned with the EMA: Group them = Large UFO = Entry

We look for ally UFOs on the Edge timeframe that envelop the 9-EMA value on the common timeframe and, therefore ,combine the indirect force of a common indicator (likely to draw more orders into the market) and direct forces of UFOs that are orders that are already there, and likely to push or turn price in the direction of the UFOs.

If there are UFOs overlapping each other and one or more of them envelop the EMA, then we would group them together to make one trade, using the reference price from the one closest to current price for our entry, and place our stop beyond the reference price that is furthest away from current price.

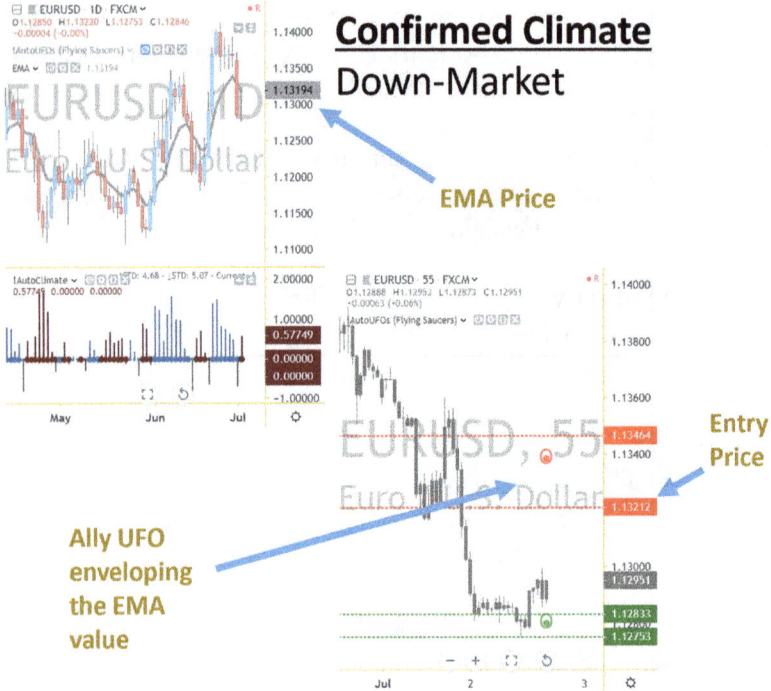

Confirmed Climate
Down-Market

EMA Price

Entry Price

Ally UFO enveloping the EMA value

Ally UFOs enveloping the EMA value

Entry Price (+2 pips)

EMA Price

<u>Confirmed Climate</u>
Up-Market

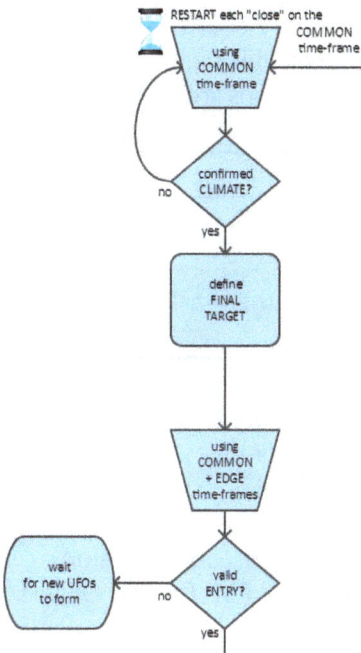

So far, this is the part of the process we have completed, and the sections of the flowchart that we've gone through:

At this point, we now know what trade direction we are going in, what our final target price would be and what our entry price is. The next step is to define our Stop Loss price.

TRADING METHODOLOGY: Stop Loss

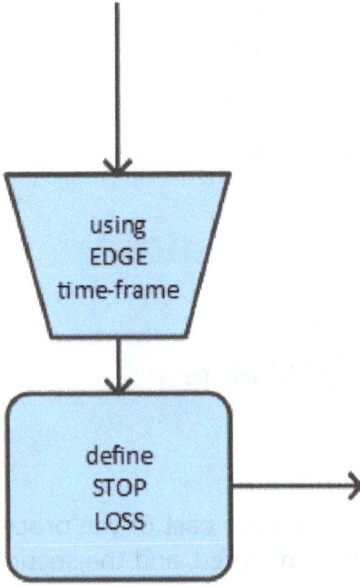

This step is probably the easiest of all as we will be using the same timeframe where we see the entry UFO and using the reference values given to easily work out our stop-loss value.

Remember, we always, always, always use stops. This step is extremely important to make sure that your risk is managed and that you are not exposed to severe losses that could occur as a result of unexpected market movements. When we are long, stop-losses are sell orders. When we are short, stop-losses are buy orders. This slightly changes the way calculations are made.

using
EDGE
time-frame

define
STOP
LOSS

Timeframe	EDGE
Tools	AutoUFOs® app
Aim	This step consists of deciding a specific value to be used as a STOP LOSS in case the Market moves against the Trade
Action	Stay with the Edge timeframe with AutoUFOs® on and identify the "extreme" location of your selected UFO or grouped UFOs chosen for entry The Stop Loss will be placed five Pips beyond this value to produce an additional protective cushion (remember to add two additional Pips for Buy Orders as they execute using the Ask Price)

	• The Stop Loss location falls between UFOs (white space in the chart): Use this value as the Stop Loss value
Possible Outcomes	• The Stop Loss location falls within some other UFO or UFOs: Group them together (treat them like a large UFO) and redefine the Stop Loss value according to the above rules making sure that the Stop Loss value falls in between UFOs (white space in the chart)

The "Extreme Value" that is the reference price for the stop is the value of the UFO that is furthest from current price. That would be the higher number on a red (sell) UFO and the lower number on a green (buy) UFO. We need to add some wiggle room to that value to give the trade some room to move before stopping us out. This avoids being stopped out by only a Pip or two, only to see price turn immediately and go in your direction (which can be extremely frustrating!).

If we use a green (buy) UFO for Entry, then we are going long and buying to enter the position. This means our exits, either for profit or loss, will be sell orders. Our stop-loss in this case is the sell order below our entry, intended to get us out of the trade for a predetermined and managed loss. In the case of going long, we take the reference number on the buy UFO that is furthest from current price (the lower number) and subtract five Pips.

If your reference values for the buy UFO are 1.9875 - 1.9855, then the entry would become 1.9877 (remember that we add two Pips to all buy orders), and the stop would become 1.9850 (five Pips below the reference value)

If we use a red (sell) UFO for entry, then we are going short and selling to enter the position. This means our exits, either for profit or loss, will be buy orders. When shorting, our stop-loss is the buy order that will go above our entry, intended to buy back and get us out of the trade for a small and predetermined loss. If our stop-loss is a buy order then then we must add two Pips, but we also need to add the wiggle room (five pips) given for stops. Our stop-loss in the case of shorting would now be seven Pips above the extreme reference value.

If your reference values for the sell UFO are 0.7195 - 0.7218, then the entry would stay at 0.7195 (it is a sell order, we do not need to alter this if it's an entry or target price), and the stop-loss would become 0.7225 (seven Pips higher than the reference value).

If the entry UFO is close to another ally UFO then sometimes, once you've added the wiggle room, the stop location will fall inside the other UFO. This means that we would be getting out of a trade while it has probability of still going our way due to the presence of ally buy or sell orders.

If we expect UFOs to turn price, then to have a stop loss within one could mean we get stopped out and then see price turn our way. For this reason, we would place our stop loss beyond the UFO in which our stop loss fell, grouping the two UFOs together, to create a large UFO zone. The entry for the trade will be using the entry UFO, using the reference price that is closer to current price (lower number for sell UFOs, higher number for buy UFOs) and the stop would be using the UFO that the stop-loss fell in, using the reference price that is further away from current price (the higher number for sell UFOs, the lower number for buy UFOs).

The easy way to summarize this is to say that the stop needs to be in the white space, i.e., not within a UFO.

Confirmed Climate
Down-Market

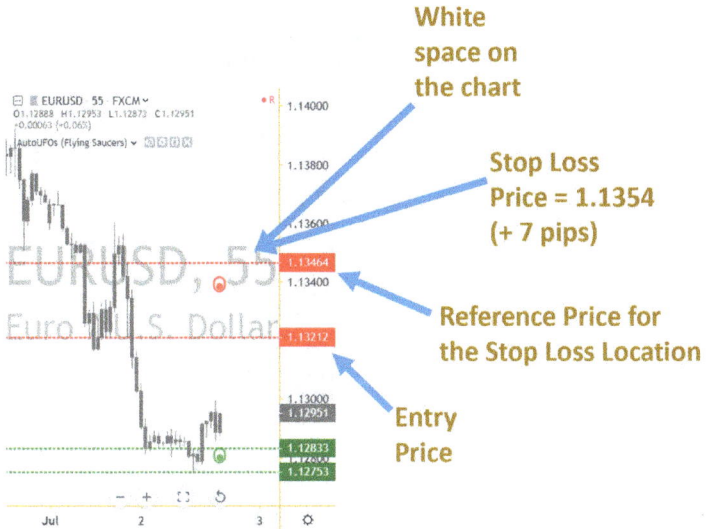

White space on the chart

Stop Loss Price = 1.1354 (+ 7 pips)

Reference Price for the Stop Loss Location

Entry Price

Confirmed Climate
Up-Market

Entry Price

Reference Price for the Stop Loss Location

White space on the chart

Stop Loss Price = 1.8088 (-5 pips)

We are now up to this point in the flowchart:

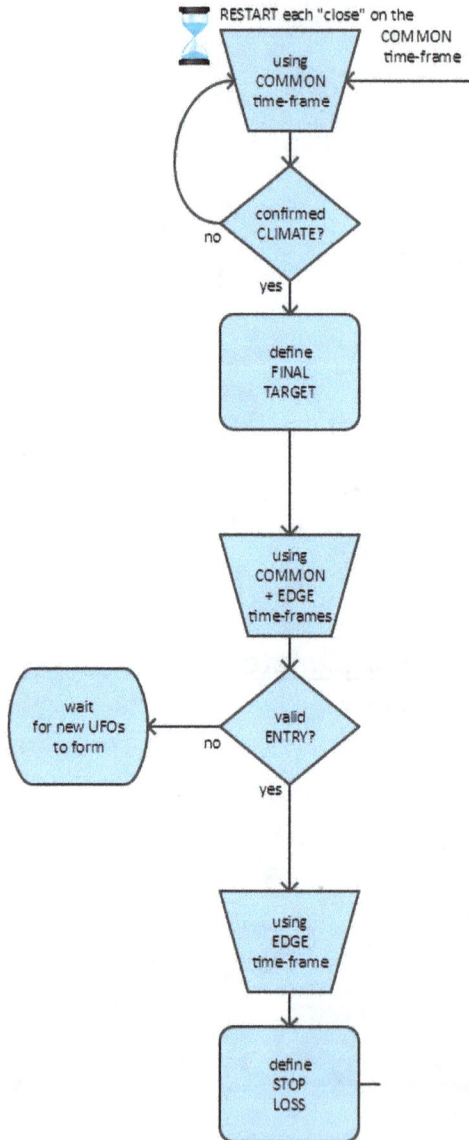

We now have our Entry, Stop and Final Target. The next step is to calculate the risk and size of the trade.

TRADING METHODOLOGY: Risk and Size

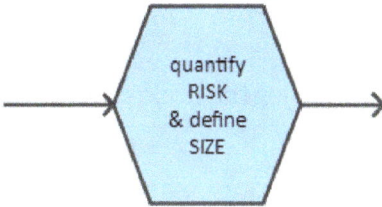

This step will be an objective calculation, but the definition of the "desired" risk will be subjective to the individual trader. Remember that this value should be no more than 2% of your trading account but that it should be a number that you are comfortable risking.

Timeframe	Irrelevant
Tools	TradingView Order Panel
Aim	This step consists of calculating the right Size for the Trade to achieve the desired Risk without surpassing it
Action	Keeping the Trade Size formula in mind, input the key parameters in the TradingView Order Panel (BUY/SELL, Entry, Stop Loss, Target and "desired" Trade Risk) Get the Trade Size by rounding down the resulting Unit value Convert the Trade Size value to the MT5 format (divide it by 100,000)
Possible Outcomes	• The Trade Size does not exceed the available capital: Time to Trade • The Trade Size exceeds the available capital: Find an alternative Trade

The risk percentage needs to stay as consistent as possible with every trade unless you have a specific rule that allows you to change it, such as 50% of normal risk, if taking a trade that is beyond the ideal climate sustainability stats. Otherwise, your calculation for trade size will always be for the same percentage of your account. Your desired risk should never be surpassed so, sometimes, you will risk your exact desired amount, but other times it may be slightly less to keep under your maximum desired risk.

We can calculate our trade size manually by using the trade size formula:

$$Trade\ Size = \frac{Ab \times R\%}{ES \times \frac{Mv}{mF}}$$

Confirmed Down Climate

- Stop Loss: 1.1354
- Short Entry: 1.1321
- ES = 0.0033
- Mv = 0.10 per micro-lot (EURUSD)
- mF = 0.0001

$$Trade\ Size = \frac{Ab \times R\%}{ES \times \frac{Mv}{mF}} =$$

$$\frac{\$5,000 \times 1\%}{0.0033 \times \frac{0.10}{0.0001}} = 15\ micro\text{-}lots$$

Confirmed Up Climate

- Long Entry: 1.8113
- Stop Loss: 1.8088
- ES = 0.0025
- Mv = 0.0684 per micro-lot (GBPAUD)
- mF = 0.0001

$$Trade\ Size = \frac{Ab \times R\%}{ES \times \frac{Mv}{mF}} =$$

$$\frac{\$5,000 \times 1\%}{0.0025 \times \frac{0.0684}{0.0001}} = 29\ micro\text{-}lots$$

Both of these examples assume an account balance of $5,000 and a desired trade risk of 1%. We would need to know the multiplier value (Mv) and minimum fluctuation (mF) of the Currency Pair that we're trading in order to calculate this accurately. Every Currency Pair that is not a Yen Pair will have a mF of 0.0001, but all Yen Pairs will have a mF of 0.01. The Mv will change per Currency Pair and also be dependent on the Currency that the trading account is held in. If you manually calculate your trade size, you will need to make sure that you know what these numbers are for your calculations.

Although it wouldn't be wrong to manually calculate our trade size, it is an unnecessarily lengthy process, which is likely to bring about human error. We would instead recommend using the TradingView order panel to calculate your trade size so that all you need to input is your entry and stop prices and desired trade risk; all other values are known and programmed into TradingView and all calculations are handled for you:

Confirmed Climate
Down-Market

This is the same EURUSD short example as before but required much less of a process for the individual trader and is, therefore, likely to be more accurate (less chance of mistakes). Whatever number of units TradingView comes back with, always round down to the closest 1,000. In this example 15,151 become 15,000 (15 micro-lots)

Confirmed Climate
Up-Market

In this same GBPAUD example, TradingView has calculated that the units needed for the desired risk is 29,241. We will round this down to 29,000 (29 micro-lots).

We are now up to this point in the flowchart, having completed and confirmed all steps along the way:

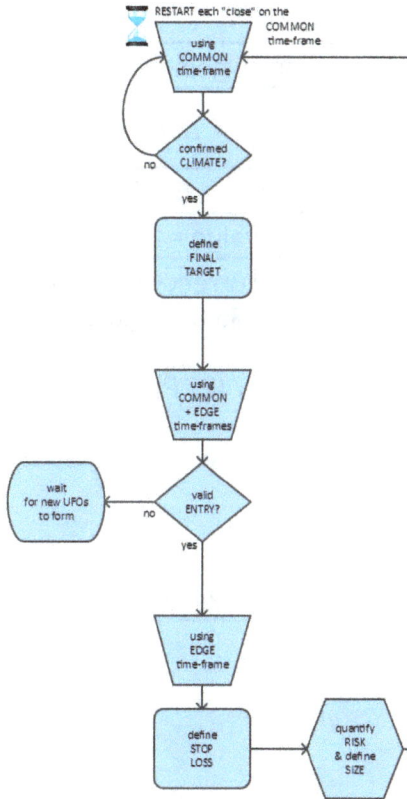

ALTERNATIVE CURRENCY PAIR EXAMPLE

The EURCAD is used below to demonstrate the Size calculation. The steps of the calculation would be the same for every Currency Pair traded, where the ES would be calculated per trade and the Mv and mF would be different, depending on the Currency Pair being traded:

Mv = this will change per currency pair

mF = for all JPY currency pairs, then the mF will be 0.01, for all other majors and minors, then the mF is 0.0001

Style of Trader	IntraDay
Climate	Focusing on going Short
Define Final Target	Final Target = 1.5627
Entry	Entry Price = 1.5775
Stop	Stop-loss value = 1.5802
Risk and Size	Assumed currency pair of EURCAD, Account balance of $5,000 and desired risk of 1% ($50) ES = 0.0027 (27 Pips) Mv = 0.0759 per micro-lot mF = 0.0001 Trade Size = 24 micro-lots

$$Trade\ Size = \frac{Ab \times R\%}{ES \times \frac{Mv}{mF}} =$$

$$\frac{\$5,000 \times 1\%}{0.0027 \times \frac{0.0759}{0.0001}} = 24\ micro\text{-}lots$$

SELL		BUY
1.56125	0.7	1.56132

MARKET	LIMIT	STOP

Order Price

1.57750 ∨	Bid + 1625 ∨
Absolute	Ticks

Quantity

24 368 ▦	50.00	0.05
Units	USD Risk	% Risk

☐ Take Profit		Stop Loss ☑
75.0	Pips	27.0
1.56851	Price	1.58020
5.70	USD	50.00
0.01	%	0.05

Once we have our trade direction, entry, stop and final target prices, as well as our trade size, then the next step is to define our safety target.

TRADING METHODOLOGY: Safety Targets

The Safety Target could be optional but we would strongly recommend using it as a fixed part of your trading methodology. The reason for this is the clue in the name "safety." Not using Safety Targets will put you at greater risk.

Using Safety Targets is a way of scaling out of our trades, taking profits once price moves in our favor a little bit, to secure a small amount of profit just in case price turns against us before it reaches our Final Target. If you were to only have a Final Target and not have a Safety Target as well, then if price were to move against you after already going in your favor for a little bit, you would give back all of the profits that you would have seen in your account and could even end up losing on the trade, even though you were right for a while.

Let's say you follow the methodology and you find a good trade to go long, you set up your entry and stop, define your size, etc., and have one single target, 5:1 away from your entry. If price were to go 4:1, but then turn against you and go all the way to your stop, then instead of making any money, you would lose on this trade. This can be psychologically difficult, leading you to break the rules and not be consistent in your approach.

The further away the Final Target, the more likely this is to happen: the higher the Reward-to-Risk ratio, the lower the probability. If your target is very far away, then price would need to continue moving in that direction for longer to reach the target price. The longer price needs to move in a particular direction, the less likely it is to continue to do that, as many things can happen that could change the direction of price. New orders could come into the market that change its direction or the climate could change and push price against you.

Although high-reward trades are appealing, they would often lack the same probability as lower-reward trades.

As we explored at the start of the book, balance is key. Safety targets are a way of finding balance. If you have a safety target, then as soon as price moves 1:1 in your favor, you will bank some of the profit. This way, if price goes anywhere up until your target but fails to hit your target price and then comes back against you and hits your stop, the worst that happens is that you break even on the trade. This reduces risk and decreases the probability of losing the trade.

Timeframe	Irrelevant
Tools	Calculator/Spreadsheet
Aim	This step consists of calculating an intermediate Target price where to scale out (close) 50% of the Trade Size to remove the Risk of the Trade entirely
Action	Collect the Entry and Stop Loss values from the prior Steps in order to calculate the vertical distance between them (ES) For Longs, take the Entry and add ES → Safety Target = Entry + ES For Shorts, take the Entry and subtract ES → Safety Target = Entry – ES Be ready to close 50% of the Trade Size at that point
Possible Outcomes	• The Safety Target falls somewhere between the Entry and the Final Target: Time to Trade • The Safety Target is located beyond the Final Target: The Final Target is too close and the Trade should be ignored; find an alternative Trade

Confirmed Climate
Down-Market

Stop Loss: 1.1354
Short Entry: 1.1321
ES = 0.0033

Safety Target = 1.1288

**Resulting
Trade Size**

- **50% is 7,575.5**
- **Rounding down is 7,000**
- **7,000 for Safety Target**
- **7,000 for Final Target**
            = 0.07 in MT5
    (7,000/100,000)

FX:EURUSD, PAPER TRADING		
SELL 1.11236	0.1	BUY 1.11237

MARKET	LIMIT	STOP

Order Price

1.13210	Bid + 1974
Absolute	Ticks

Quantity

15 151		50.00	0.05
Units		$ Risk	% Risk

☑ Take Profit	1.94	Stop Loss ☑
64.0	Pips	33.0
1.12570	Price	1.13540
96.97	$	50.00
0.10	%	0.05

Time in Force WEEK

SELL 15 151 FX:EURUSD @ 1.13210 LMT

The safety target is going to be close to our entry so the probability of reaching it will be relatively high. We will still have our final target waiting, ideally wanting to capture all the movement and make decent profits, but we understand this isn't as likely. Having both targets, allows us to capitalize on high probability, as well as high-reward trades. If the Final Target falls beyond the Safety Target, then the Final Target – and therefore the trade – is valid. If the Final Target falls between the entry and Safety Target, then the trade would lack suitable reward opportunities to be valid.

Calculating the ES and then either adding it to entries for long positions, or subtracting it from entries for short positions, is essentially calculating where a 1:1 target would be. Taking 50% of our position off at 1:1 means that we have now banked in profit the same amount of money that is still at risk. If price goes against us and stops us out after hitting the safety target, we won't win on the trade, nor will we lose; we will have a breakeven trade.

Confirmed Climate
Up-Market

FX:GBPAUD, PAPER TRADING

Long Entry: 1.8113
Stop Loss: 1.8088
ES = 0.0025

SELL		BUY
1.88148	1.1	1.88159

MARKET   LIMIT   STOP

Order Price

1.81130   Ask - 7029

Absolute   Ticks

Quantity

Safety Target = 1.8138

29 241		50.00	0.05
Units		$ Risk	% Risk

Resulting Trade Size

☑ Take Profit   14.12   Stop Loss ☑

353.0	Pips	25.0
1.84660	Price	1.80880
706.00	$	50.00
0.71	%	0.05

Time in Force WEEK

- **50% is 14,620.5**
- **Rounding down is 14,000**
- **14,000 for Safety Target**
- **14,000 for Final Target**
    = 0.14 in MT5
    (14,000/100,000)

BUY 29 241 FX:GBPAUD @ 1.81130 LMT

When looked at as Reward-to-Risk ratios, if we were to take a trade with just a final target, then a target of 5:1 means risking "1" (which will be worth your desired trade risk) to make five times that number. For example, risking $50 to make $250, or $10 to make $50, or $200 to make $1,000. When using a Safety Target, we split the "1" in half and risk 0.5 to make 0.5 (1:1 target) and risk the other 0.5 on our Final Target (0.5 to make 2.5 = 5:1 target). The overall profit becomes 3:1 (0.5 + 2.5), assuming both targets are reached. If only the Safety Target is reached, the outcome is overall 0 (+0.5 -0.5)

Let's say you are going long:

- Entry = 1.5060
- Stop-loss = 1.5040
- ES = 20 Pips
- Total size of trade = 38 micro-lots
- Safety Target = 1.5080 (20 Pips above Entry) [19 micro-lots]
- Final Target = 1.5160 (100 Pips above Entry= 5:1 trade) [19 micro-lots]

Let's assume a total risk of $50 so each target has its own risk of $25; each set of 19 micro-lots equals $25. If price hits the Safety Target, but then turns and hits the stop, this is the outcome:

- Safety Target reached = 19 micro-lots sold (+$25)
- Stop-loss hit = 19 micro-lots sold (-$25)
- Overall P/L = $0

The benefit of this is that the trade does not become a loss even though price never reached our Final Target and hit our stop-loss. However, there is a downside: Taking 50% of our profits at 1:1 and 50% profits at our Final Target (which could be any distance away) will reduce the total profit if the Final Target was to be reached. Using the same case as before:

- Entry = 1.5060
- Stop-loss = 1.5040
- ES = 20 Pips
- Total size of trade = 38 micro-lots
- Total risk of the trade = $50
- Safety Target = 1.5080 (20 pips above Entry) [19 micro-lots]
- Final Target = 1.5160 (100 Pips above Entry= 5:1 trade) [19 micro-lots]

If both targets were to be hit, this would be the outcome:

- Safety Target reached = 19 micro-lots sold (+$25)
- Final Target reached = 19 micro-lots sold (+$125)
- Overall P/L = $150

Although the Final Target was 5:1 away, the total profit was not 5:1, as half the profit was taken at 1:1:

- Total risk of the trade = $50
- Overall Profit = $150
- Overall Reward-to-Risk achieved = 3:1

If the Safety Target had not been taken and the trade had simply been "all in all out" at the 5:1 Final Target, then the overall outcome would be:

- Total risk of the trade = $50
- Overall profit = $250
- Overall Reward-to-Risk achieved = 5:1

When trying to obtain balance, there will always be sacrifices that need to be made: if we want to capture higher rewards, then we risk losing more often in pursuit of those greater profits. If we want higher probability and fewer losses, then we will need to accept smaller overall profits when we are right.

There is no right or wrong when deciding whether to use Safety Targets. This is up to individual traders to decide based on psychology, trading plans, risk tolerance, etc. Some will prefer taking greater profits off the table less often, others will prefer taking smaller profits off the table more frequently. For most newer traders, it is easier to make smaller profits more frequently to build confidence in what they are doing and to make it easier psychologically.

Some more experienced traders may choose to ignore the Safety Targets as they are more comfortable to take more frequent losses in exchange for greater profits realized.

The most important thing is to be consistent. If you choose to use Safety Targets, use them all the time. If you choose not to use them, do not use them. Consistent action leads to consistent results; splitting risk into two targets sometimes, but not all the time, will produce inconsistent results and it would be hard to know what's working for you and what isn't.

Safety Targets by nature are close to our entries, which means not only do they get reached more frequently, but that should happen relatively quickly. Half of our position is taken off within a short amount of time; this frees up capital and margin to place other trades in parallel. If you are out of risk on trade No. 1, then you can place trade No. 2 without potentially adding too much to your overall risk exposure. This is especially helpful for traders who wish to be relatively active and run multiple trades in parallel.

We are now at the following step in the flowchart, having completed all tasks along the way:

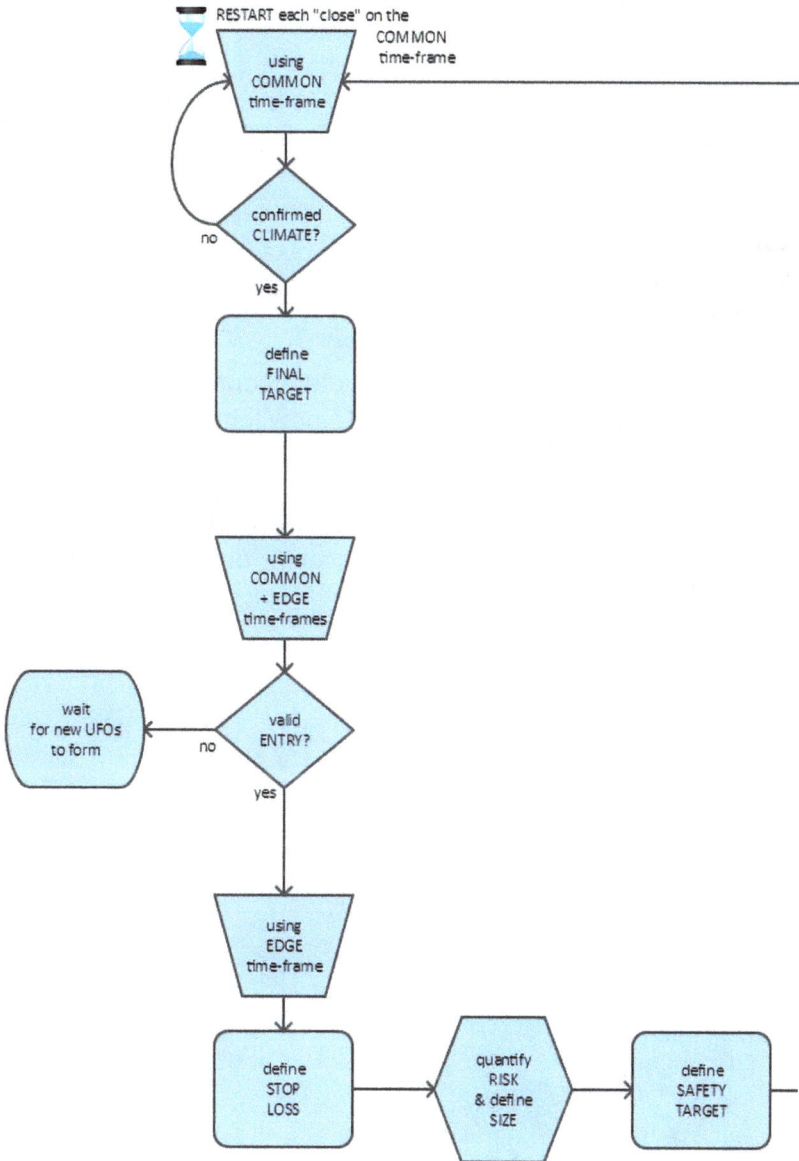

ORDER TYPES

Placing Orders is a critical part in Trading as this is how we provide our Trading Platforms with specific instructions for Trade Execution:

- When to Enter (what Price)
- When to Exit (what Price)
- Which Quantities
- Which Duration

The quantities refer to how many shares, lots, contracts, etc., you would like to buy or sell. The duration refers to how long you want the order to last for. When you give an instruction to your platform, you can make those orders last forever, or dictate a specific time that it would expire. For example, a "Day" order is automatically canceled at the end of the trading day. A "GTC" or "Good Till Canceled" order is valid until you manually choose to cancel it.

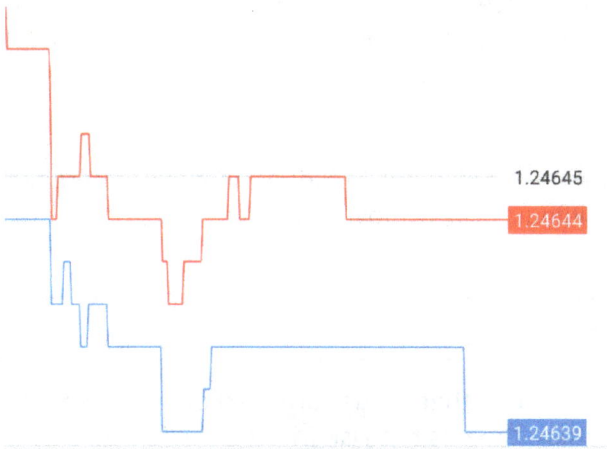

Basic Order Types

Market Orders:

- Accept any available Price in the Market
- Buyers pay the Ask price
- Sellers receive the Bid price
- Slippage may occur in illiquid or fast-moving Markets

Limit Orders:

- Specify a desired Price which may or may not be available in the Market (fills are not guaranteed)
- Buyers pay the Bid price or better
- Sellers receive the Ask price or better

Limit orders allow us to set a specific price for our desired buy or sell, meaning we can receive our desired price as sellers (the Ask price) and buy the desired price as buyers (the Bid price). This comes at a cost of not always being filled on our orders. We use limit orders for entries and targets to increase probabilities of getting a better price when we are filled.

Market orders guarantee a fill but leave us more vulnerable to slippage, especially in illiquid or fast-moving markets.

Stop Orders

The Stop-loss Orders that we use are market orders so this can lead to losing more than the desired risk in certain situations. It is rare but it does happen.

Stop Orders execute only when a triggering condition is met:

Stop Market Orders:

- Execute at any available Price in the Market once a triggering Price condition is met (Stop Price)
- Normally used to close losing Trades and manage risk
- Known as "Stop Loss"

Stop Limit Orders:

- Execute at a desired Price once an additional Price condition (Stop Price) is met (fills are not guaranteed)
- Should NEVER be used to protect trades or manage risk
- Not common, could be used to enter Trades (breakouts)

It may be confusing to see that stops can be used to enter trades. If you think of a stop more like an order that needs to meet a condition, it can be easier to understand.

If we are using a Stop Market Order, then price has to meet a certain condition (price level) before a market order can be used. We are instructing our platforms to only send a market-order to the market when the price of what we are trading reaches a certain point (stop price). The stop-loss order will then send a market order to guarantee a fill even if we do have more probability of slippage. Remember, market orders will guarantee a fill as they will accept any available price in the market.

If we used a Stop Limit Order, then price still needs to meet a condition before the limit order is used, but as it would be a limit order that would be sent, the fill would not be guaranteed. However, if filled, the filled price is likely to be better than the market order alternative. These types of orders are used in other styles of trading not covered in this book, and we NEVER use them for stop-losses, due to the lack of a guaranteed fill.

- **Limit Orders** = Used for entries and targets
- **Stop-Market Orders** = Used for stop-losses

Most platforms will automatically default to this format of order types.

BRACKET ORDERS

Basic Order Types are rarely used in Professional Trading. Proper Trading implies defining entries and exits altogether before executing a trade and, therefore, a proper way to trade is to always use Bracket Orders where Stops and Targets are always defined and sent together with the Entry Order, at the same time. This eliminates the chance of being caught in a trade with no stop or with no target, which would imply a lack of using a structured and consistent plan.

A Bracket Order is a combination where three Basic Orders are linked and sent at the same time:

- A Limit Order to initiate the trade (Entry)
- A Stop Market Order to close the trade for a loss if the market was not to behave as expected (Stop Loss)
- A Limit Order to close the trade for a profit if the market was to move as expected (Target)

Going Long with a Bracket

This example uses the MT5 mobile app. A similar process would be done on a desktop or web-based platform:

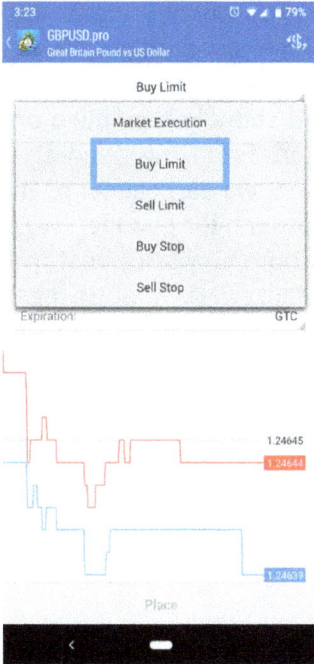

Step #1: Click on Buy Limit

This will open up a separate window, where you will then be able to input your Entry, Stop and Target prices as well as your trade duration and trade size.

Step #2: Input the size (lots)

Step #3: Input the Entry price

Step #4: Input the Stop Loss price

Step #5: Input the Target price

Step #6: Confirm duration is "GTC" (Good Till Cancelled)

Step #7: Complete by clicking on "Place"

Your App will now show you that you have a pending bracket order. If the order were to be filled, it would show in the "filled orders" section. From the pending order section, we can cancel or modify our orders; for instance, we could alter our entry price or stop loss if we realize we've made a mistake.

Going Short with a Bracket

This example uses the MT5 mobile app. A similar process would be done on a desktop or web-based platform:

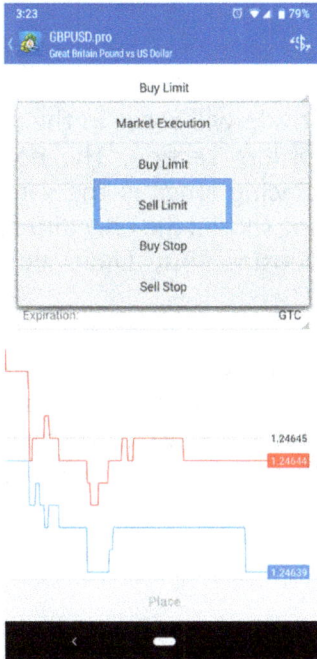

Step #1: Click on Sell Limit

This will be the same as the instance before (where we clicked Buy Limit) in that it will open up a separate window where you will then be able to input your Entry, Stop and Target prices as well as your trade duration and trade size, but will be setting up your trade to be short instead of long.

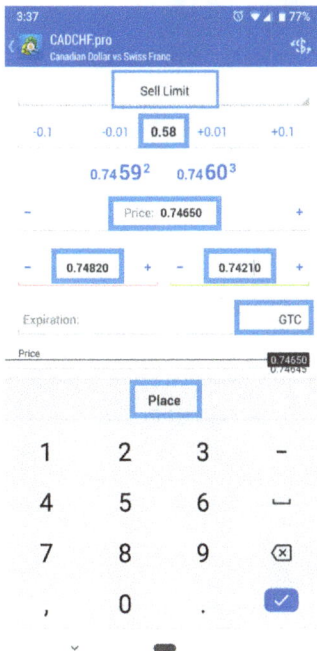

Step #2: Input the size (lots)

Step #3: Input the Entry price

Step #4: Input the Stop Loss price

Step #5: Input the Target price

Step #6: Confirm duration is "GTC" (Good Till Cancelled)

Step #7: Complete by clicking on "Place"

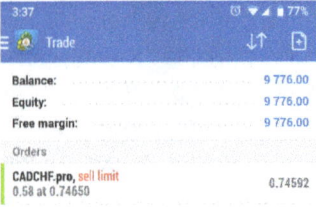

The trade will show in the pending orders section. The process for placing longs is the same as placing shorts; the only difference is choosing "Buy Limit" or "Sell Limit."

Now that we understand different order types and how to place bracket orders, we can get back to the flowchart and the next step.

TRADING METHODOLOGY: Execute the Trade

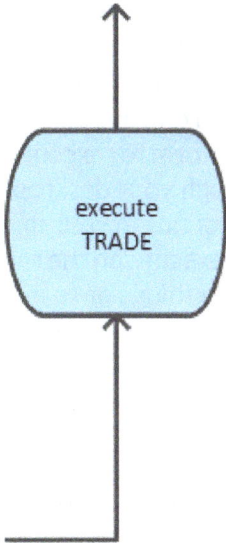

execute
TRADE

We started by identifying a confirmed climate that is sustainable (answering Question No. 1, "Should I be long, short, or do nothing?"). We used AutoClimate™ on our Common Timeframe to aid us in this analysis. We defined our Final Target using AutoUFOs® and then we went on to answer Question No. 2, "Where is the best price to buy or sell?" We found a valid entry using AutoUFOs® on the Edge Timeframe and the 9-EMA on the Common Timeframe. We defined our Entry and Stop-Loss prices before quantifying the risk and defining the size of the trade. We then calculated our safety target. We now have all the information we need to execute the trade

Timeframe	Irrelevant
Tools	Mobile MT5 Platform
Aim	This step consists of placing two Bracket Orders in a way where the Trading platform can guard and take care of executing the Trade with minimal human interaction
Action	Place 2 Bracket Orders with 50% of the Trade Size each The 1st Bracket would use: Entry / Stop Loss / Safety Target The 2nd Bracket would use: Entry (same) / Stop Loss (same) / Final Target

Possible Outcomes	• The Trade Size does not exceed the available capital: Time to Trade
	• The Trade Size exceeds the available capital: Find an alternative Trade

The orders are better placed using a mobile MT5 platform rather than using the same technology that you used to analyze the trade. If you do your analysis on a web-based or desktop platform on your laptop or computer, we would recommend using a mobile platform for execution. It is not critical as you can, of course, execute through your desktop or web-based platform too, but it separates the two actions in your mind. If you complete the analysis process and then go to execute on the same platform and device, you may be tempted to change things or to enter as you see price move. If you have all your prices for your entry, stop and targets and execute on a mobile platform, you will more likely simply enter the numbers and execute the trade as it needs to be executed.

Ultimately, this is up to the individual trader; there certainly isn't an issue to execute on the same device and many may not find it difficult to stay disciplined with their executions. But if you are newer to trading, or know that you are a person who is likely to get tempted into entering a trade impulsively, one efficient way to manage that is to execute on a different device.

The demonstrations in this book are using the MT5 mobile app. The process would be extremely similar no matter the broker used, including MT4 brokers or even brokers that use their own proprietary trading platforms.

Most trading platforms will require us to enter two separate orders for our trades: one for the Safety Target and one for the Final Target. Although we would know that our Long trade is one trade with two targets, and our Short trade is one trade with two targets, most trading platforms will show each bracket order as separate trades or orders so you will see two separate orders for one trade in your "orders" section.

GBPAUD Long Execution

Example Trade Parameters:
Final Target: 1.8466
Safety Target: 1.8138
Long Entry: 1.8113
Stop Loss: 1.8088
Trade Size: 29 micro-lots

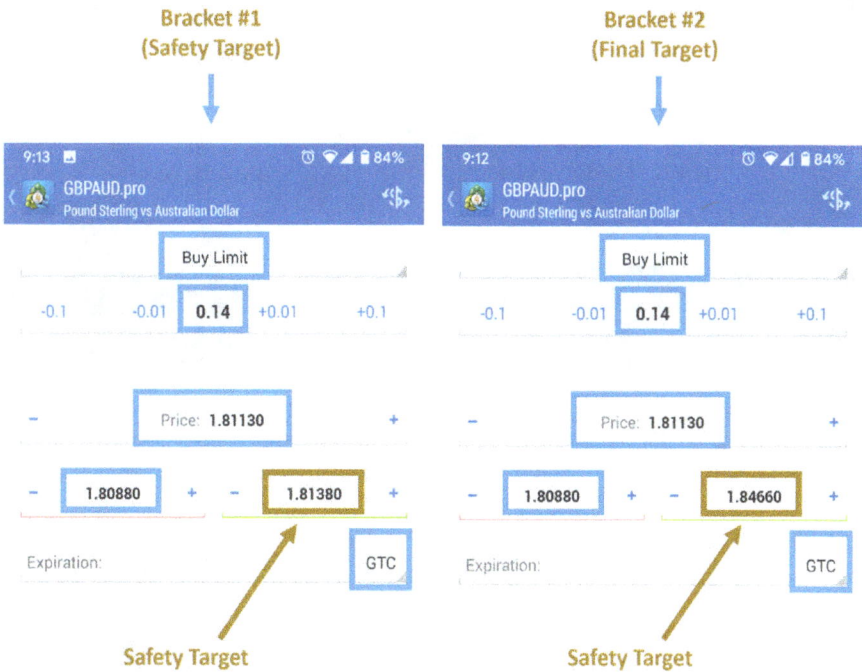

Bracket #1
(Safety Target)

Bracket #2
(Final Target)

The process is the same when placing the safety target and the final target as separate brackets:

#1: The Order type is the same (Buy Limit)
#2: The Trade Size is the same (50% of total risk each)
#3: The Entry Price is the same
#4: The Stop Loss Order is the same
#5: The duration is the same (always GTC, "Good Till Cancelled")

#6: The Target is the parameter that changes – one will reflect the Safety Target price and one will reflect the Final Target price

EURUSD Short Execution

Example Trade Parameters:
Stop Loss: 1.1354
Short Entry: 1.1321
Safety Target: 1.1288
Final Target: 1.1023
Trade Size: 15 micro-lots

**Bracket #1
(Safety Target)**

**Bracket #2
(Final Target)**

7:55 ⏰ ▼◢ ▪ 55%	7:55 ⏰ ▼◢ ▪ 55%
EURUSD.pro — Euro vs US Dollar	EURUSD.pro — Euro vs US Dollar
Sell Limit	Sell Limit
-0.1 -0.01 **0.07** +0.01 +0.1	-0.1 -0.01 **0.07** +0.01 +0.1
– Price: **1.13210** +	– Price: **1.13210** +
– 1.13540 + – 1.12880 +	– 1.13540 + – 1.10230 +
Expiration: GTC	Expiration: GTC

Safety Target   **Safety Target**

The process is exactly the same when executing a short trade, apart from changing the order type to "Sell Limit" instead of "Buy Limit." We still place two orders, one for each target (Safety and Final). The Order Type, Trade Size, Entry, Stop and Duration will be the same for each order; the only parameter that changes is the Target price.

At this point, we have completed the first section of the flowchart:

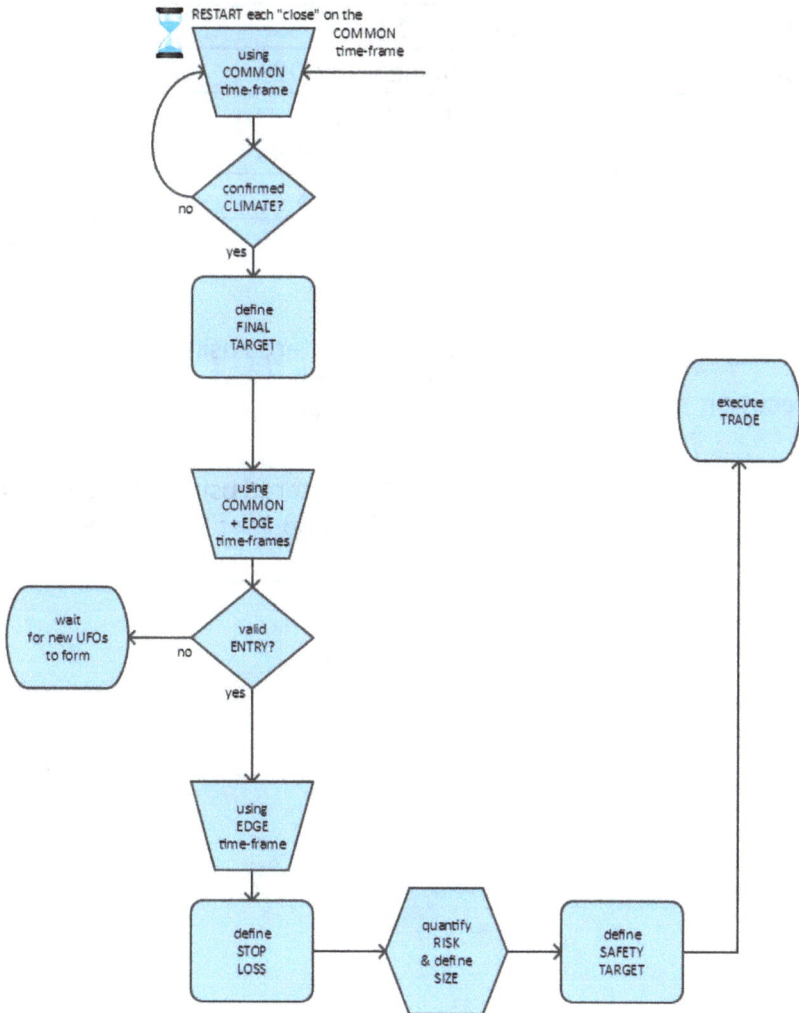

ALTERNATIVE CURRENCY PAIR EXAMPLE

Building on the prior EURCAD trade example, now including Execution:

Style of Trader	Intra-day
Climate	Focusing on going Short
Define Final Target	Final Target = 1.5627
Entry	Entry Price = 1.5775
Stop	Stop-loss value = 1.5802
Risk and Size	ES = 0.0027 (27 Pips) Trade Size = 24 micro-lots
Safety Target	Safety Target = 1.5748
Execution	Switch to mobile MT5 platform and go to place an order One bracket order entered using 12 micro-lots with Entry 1.5775, Stop-Loss 1.5802 and target 1.5748 (Safety Target) One bracket order entered using 12 micro-lots with Entry 1.5775, Stop-Loss 1.5802 and target 1.5627 (Final Target)

TRADING METHODOLOGY: Manage the Trade

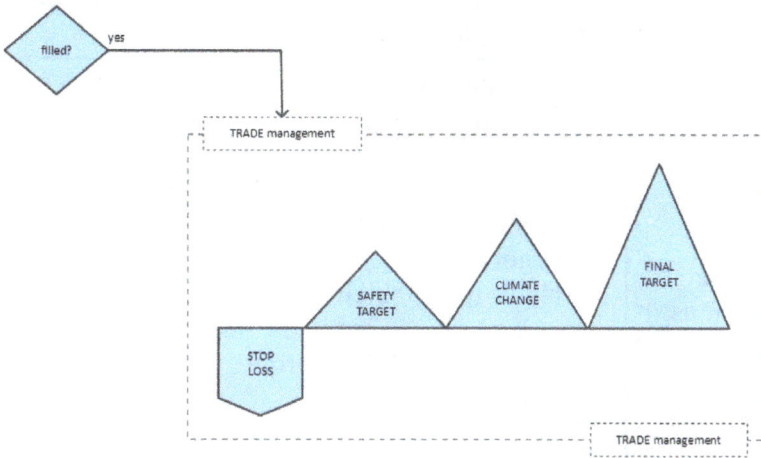

Managing the trade refers to what you need to do during the life of the trade once it's already filled. This may include some additional steps or rules that help you lock in profit, further manage your risk and adapt in accordance with new probabilities.

Doing nothing is okay too, provided the balance of risk, probability and reward is still valid for the trade. If you enter the trade and hit your target relatively quickly, then there is nothing to do during the length of the trade apart from enjoy the profits. If you enter the trade and hit your Stop Loss relatively quickly, then there is nothing to do throughout the trade's lifespan apart from accept the loss. In both cases, we would log the trade in order to keep a record from which we can learn and grow as traders, but there is no additional action required during the length of this type of trade.

This is not always the case and, as good traders, we need to be aware of what we may need to do once the trade entry has been filled.

Timeframe	EDGE + COMMON
Tools	AutoUFOs® + AutoClimate™ apps
Aim	This step consists of monitoring the Trade where additional optional Trade Management techniques could be implemented
Action	Allow the Trade to happen according to the pre-defined Trade Management Rules
Possible Outcomes	• Reaching the Final Target (maximum profit - "Smooth Target") • Not Reaching the Final Target because of a Change of Climate (may have reached the Safety Target prior to it) and exiting somewhere in the middle (profitable) • Reaching the Safety Target and then reaching the Stop Loss (break-even) • Reaching the Stop Loss without hitting the Safety Target first (unprofitable)

As we have pre-programmed our targets and stops and we are using advanced platforms, then most of the trade management is taken care of for us by automated orders. A lot of the time we will simply need to step back and allow the trade to do what it will do. However, much you stare at the screen, you won't be able to coax price up or down and you don't want to meddle in a trade and change your plan as it's happening.

If you have a plan, stick to it. As long as everything is still lining up, you don't need to interfere and, potentially, get out of the trade before you could have hit your Final Target. In some cases, reaching your targets will be relatively smooth:

SMOOTH TARGET

Further Trade Management techniques were not really needed in this trade as Price kept moving towards the Target continuously.

Out and Climate Change

In the above image, was 1.1257 a good Final Target? What about the Climate Change that happened afterwards?

We see with hindsight that the trade went much further than the Final Target and so it would be easy to say that it would have been better to have a lower target. But we never have a crystal ball and could never know in advance that this was going to happen. We only have market data and probabilities, so if the plan was followed and the Final Target was taken where prices were likely to change direction (the closest rival UFO on the Common timeframe), this was the correct place to put the target.

The above example also shows us that the Climate changed from a confirmed down to a confirmed up somewhere in the middle of the total move. Although it happened to end up further down, a change in Climate could have signaled that price would move against the trade and potentially lead to a stop out. If the Final Target was not where it was, then a change in Climate could have wiped out all potential profits. This is why we determine in advance where we have higher probabilities to take a decent target and we lock in profits more consistently.

During the initial planning process, you may have circumstances that invalidate your trade, so you don't execute it. This logic still applies once you're in the trade. If the parameters have changed before you hit your Target, and the circumstances no longer support what would be a valid trade, then it's time to get out of the trade.

The first thing we look at to help determine if we have a valid trade is the Climate. If we have a defined upwards Climate, then we have probabilities to the upside and can therefore progress to analyzing long trades. If we have a defined downwards Climate, then we have probabilities to the downside and can therefore progress to analyzing short trades. If we are already in a trade and the Climate changes, we no longer have probabilities in our trade direction – in fact, we would have probabilities now working against us. Of course, "probable" doesn't mean "definite" and sometimes (like in the above example) price does unexpected things and moves past our predicted targets. Perhaps the Climate changes against us, but before it hits our stop it changes again to our favor.

But this is all unlikely, as it contradicts the probabilities. It may happen sometimes but not often enough to constitute a consistent approach to trading.

We are now at this point in the flowchart:

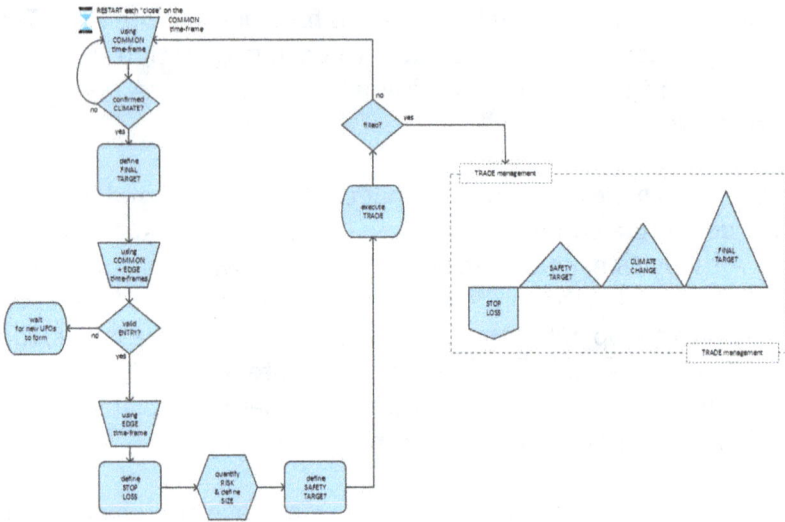

In summary, after we've analyzed, executed and been filled on the trade (Entry hit), we have a few outcomes that can happen:

- Stop-loss is hit, pre-defined risk is lost
- Trade closes as a loss
- Safety Target is hit, followed by the Stop-loss
- Trade closes as breakeven
- Safety Target is hit, followed by the Final Target, total profit collected
- Trade closes as a profit
- The Climate changes at some point between Entry and either the Stop-Loss or Target(s) being hit, trade closed manually
- Trade could close for a smaller loss than expected
- Trade could close for a smaller profit than expected

Once the trade is over, we now need to log the trade.

TRADING METHODOLOGY: Logging the Trade

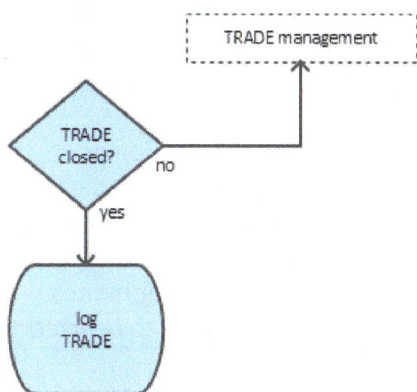

Our trade outcomes, as well as entry, stop and target prices that were filled, are all logged by our brokers electronically. But we do need our own logs too.

We keep a log of our trades on our own spreadsheets to keep a record of the methodology used and the thought process behind the trade, and to keep track of how we're doing in our trading overall. What is logged automatically by our platforms and brokers is no more than information on the prices, the time we are filled and how much was made or lost. Although we would see whether we are overall at a profit or loss, it cannot tell us what elements of our methodology are working better for us or analyze adjustments to our plan moving forward.

Timeframe	Irrelevant
Tools	Spreadsheet
Aim	This step consists of taking notes that objectively represent the outcome of the Trade to review such results to identify areas of improvement
Action	Input the Trade parameters and chart pictures in a Spreadsheet Review such results each week/month

Possible Outcomes	• The results achieved the Trader goals: Keep Trading • The results are stable but did not achieve the desired goals: Analyze and consider which changes could help (more trades, fewer trades, different timeframes, non-correlated Markets, etc.) • The results are not stable: Review the log or increase the amount of information available in it to identify the origin of the problem (emotions, not following rules, variable Trade Size, etc.); stop Trading real money and switch to paper money until the lack of consistency is proven to be fixed

There are many variables that make up a trade. Each individual market you look at, each timeframe used, any indicator utilized - these are all variables that could have an impact on the outcome of the trade. These are also things that can be analyzed if you don't see the results you want to see if you can tweak your methodology and improve your results.

If you are not making money, or are losing money, then it's best to stop trading with real money and continue practicing and learning with paper-money until you've identified the problem in your methodology.

Some of the parameters that are sensible to log on your spreadsheet:

- Dates (date placed, date triggered, date closed)
- Symbol (e.g. EURUSD, GBPJPY etc.)
- Type (stance, Long or Short)
- Risk (in Pips and in money, whichever currency your account is in)
- Reward (as with risk)
- Strategy used
- Notes on the trade (before, during and after)
- Snapshots of the trade
- Trade Grade (Did everything line up perfectly, or were there hindrances – i.e., over-extended climate or too-close rival UFOs?)

These are suggestions, but of course you can log other variables, too, which may include:

- Timeframes used
- Time of day you traded
- Correlated positions
- Other indicators applied

A trading log may look something like this:

	A	B	C	D	O	P	Q	R	S
					R:R				
1 2	Date	Symbol	Type	Qty	Risk	Reward	Result	Strategy	Notes Before Trade
30	20190515	ESM19	Short	2	-$350	$2,275	$175	UFO	Strong DOWNtrend, overlapping red UFOs on all Edge TFs. Adjusted entry to match MA.
31	20190516	CLM19	Long	2	-$60	$1,900	$0	UFO	Strong UPTrend, 2m UFO. Price retraced to MA
32	20190516	CLM19	Long	2	-$200	$2,200	$60	UFO	Strong UPTrend, overlapping green UFOs on all Edge TFs. Entry below MA.
33	20190516	ESM19	Long	2	-$225	$750	-$125	UFO	Strong UPTrend, overlapping green UFOs on Edge TFs. Entry at MA
34	20190517								
35	20190518								
36	20190519								
37	20190520								
38	20190521	ECM19	Long	2	-$40.00	$328	-$40	UFO	Strong UPTrend, overlapping Green UFOs on 2 Edge TFs. Entry at MA.
39	20190522	ESM19	Long	2	-$300	$2,038	$100	UFO	Strong UPTrend, overlapping Green UFOs on 2 Edge TFs. Entry at MA. Reactive TF also showing Green UFOs
40	20190522	ESM19	Long	2	-$225	$1,925	$100	UFO	Strong UPTrend, overlapping Green UFOs on 2 Edge TFs. Entry at MA. Reactive TF also showing Green UFOs
41	20190523								
42	20190524	ESM19	Long	2	-$500	$1,500	$100	UFO	Strong UPTrend, overlapping Green UFOs on 2 Edge TFs. Entry at MA. Reactive TF also showing Green UFOs
43	20190524	CLN19	Short	2	-$160	$310	$180	UFO	Strong DOWNtrend, SB TF UFO. Entry at MA.
44	20190525								
45	20190526								
46	20190527	CLN19	Long	2			-$60	UFO	Strong UPTrend, Green UFO on Share TFs, Entry with MA and Reactive TF
47	20190527	CLN19	Long	2			-$40	UFO	Strong UPTrend, Green UFO on Share TFs, Entry with MA and Reactive TF
48	20190528	ESM19	Long	2	-$250	$375	$375	UFO	Weak UPTrend, Green UFOs on multiple Edge TFs. No Reactive UFOs
49	20190529								
50	20190530	ESM19	Long	2	-$250	$388	$388	UFO	Strong UPTrend, Green UFO on SB Edge TF, multiple reactive UFOs

	A	B	C	D ◀	▶ O	P	Q	R	T	U
1	Date	Symbol	Type	Qty	R:R		Result	Strategy	Pictures of Chart (link)	
2					Risk	Reward			Entry	Exit
30	20190515	ESM19	Short	2	-$350	$2,275	$175	UFO	https://prntscr.com/npsoop	https://prntscr.com/npsorj https://prntscr.com/npsovc
31	20190516	CLM19	Long	2	-$60	$1,900	$0	UFO	https://prntscr.com/npt083	https://prntscr.com/npt0dy
32	20190516	CLM19	Long	2	-$200	$2,200	$60	UFO	https://prntscr.com/npt63y	https://prntscr.com/npt661
33	20190516	ESM19	Long	2	-$225	$750	-$125	UFO	https://prnt.sc/npt8vs	https://prnt.sc/npt8xm
34	20190517									
35	20190518									
36	20190519									
37	20190520									
38	20190521	ECM19	Long	2	-$40.00	$328	-$40	UFO	https://prntscr.com/nry99i	https://prntscr.com/nry9cb
39	20190522	ESM19	Long	2	-$300	$2,038	$100	UFO	https://prntscr.com/nrzdjh	https://prntscr.com/nrzdld
40	20190522	ESM19	Long	2	-$225	$1,925	$100	UFO	https://prnt.sc/nrzfg0	https://prnt.sc/nrzfir https://prnt.sc/nrzflo
41	20190523									
42	20190524	ESM19	Long	2	-$500	$1,500	$100	UFO	https://prntscr.com/nuwai1	https://prntscr.com/nuwajn
43	20190524	CLN19	Short	2	-$160	$310	$180	UFO	https://prntscr.com/nuwaps	https://prntscr.com/nuwarg
44	20190525									
45	20190526									
46	20190527	CLN19	Long	2			-$60	UFO	https://prnt.sc/ntybky	https://prnt.sc/ntybm4
47	20190527	CLN19	Long	2			-$40	UFO	https://prnt.sc/ntybky	https://prnt.sc/ntybnp
48	20190528	ESM19	Long	2	-$250	$375	$375	UFO	https://prntscr.com/nuwsw3	https://prntscr.com/nuwsxz
49	20190529									
50	20190530	ESM19	Long	2	-$250	$388	$388	UFO	https://prnt.sc/nvfzse	https://prnt.sc/nvfzzi

	Date	Symbol	Type	Qty	R:R Risk	R:R Reward	Result	Strategy	Notes After Trade
30	20190515	ESM19	Short	2	-$350	$2,275	$175	UFO	Probably one of my best trades so far. Pre-planned, adjusted per plan, entered per plan, managed per plan!
31	20190516	CLM19	Long	2	-$60	$1,900	$0	UFO	Traded according to plan, for a B/E result.
32	20190516	CLM19	Long	2	-$200	$2,200	$60	UFO	TinT prevented $2200 profit. Traded according to plan, closed trade at market due to "Time-in-Trade" rule. Trade worked out to T1, and is working its way to T2.
33	20190516	ESM19	Long	2	-$225	$750	-$125	UFO	Trade opened according to plan, but was poorly managed as I had to step away from my desk. If correctly managed it would have been closed at B/E or a small profit at 3 candles. I waited and "made up" a rule that if I get a close below the MA, I'm out, so I did it.
34	20190517								
35	20190518								
36	20190519								
37	20190520								
38	20190521	ECM19	Long	2	-$40.00	$328	-$40	UFO	Trade was a low risk, high probability trade, which ended up working a few hours later
39	20190522	ESM19	Long	2	-$300	$2,038	$100	UFO	TinT prevented a $2038 profit. Traded according to plan, closed trade at market due to TinT
40	20190522	ESM19	Long	2	-$225	$1,925	$100	UFO	Reached T1 between the 3-5 "time-in-trade" rule. Adjusted stop to below ally Green UFOs. Price reversed, conserved profit. Was unsure about stop placement in white space vs overlapping ally UFOs
41	20190523								Had a setup on CL, but price never returned to my entry
42	20190524	ESM19	Long	2	-$500	$1,500	$100	UFO	Traded according to plan, closed trade at market due to "Time-in-Trade" rule. Trade would have worked out to T1. Stop was exceeding the daily loss allowance ($500 risk)
43	20190524	CLN19	Short	2	-$160	$310	$180	UFO	TinT prevented a $160 loss. Exited trade at market
44	20190525								
45	20190526								
46	20190527	CLN19	Long	2			-$60	UFO	Price was bouncing between 60m UFOs, Got stopped on both trades the same way. There wasn't enough profit potential, so I should not have taken thes trades
47	20190527	CLN19	Long	2			-$40	UFO	
48	20190528	ESM19	Long	2	-$250	$375	$375	UFO	TinT (would have) prevented a $375 profit. Also trade was taking during the open, which can be dangerous, but I went with it as Jose was also in it. Tradestation tech. issues, had to close it at market, still profited
49	20190529								
50	20190530	ESM19	Long	2	-$250	$388	$388	UFO	TinT (would have) prevented a $388 profit. Also trade was taking during the open, which can be dangerous, but I went with it as we did the same thing yesterday

Date	Symbol	Type	Qty	R:R Risk	R:R Reward	Result	Strategy	Trade Grade	Daily Notes	Time Spent Trading (hrs)
20190515	ESM19	Short	2	-$350	$2,275	$175	UFO	A+	Taking the stop at entry saved me $, as the trend reversed	4
20190516	CLM19	Long	2	-$60	$1,900	$0	UFO	A		
20190516	CLM19	Long	2	-$200	$2,200	$60	UFO	A-	Should be more careful not to enter below the MA	3
20190516	ESM19	Long	2	-$225	$750	-$125	UFO	C+	Should not leave the desk when in an active trade. Should not "make-up" rules on the spot in the middle of a trade	
20190517									Both CL and ES in downtrend, but bouncing off of a 60M Green UFO. Sitting patiently, no trades	3
20190518									Jose with AutoUFOs session, going over trading strategies and analyses	4
20190519										
20190520									day off with family	
20190521	ECM19	Long	2	-$40.00	$328	-$40	UFO	A	Missed a trade from Jose, which he entered on the NQ	4
20190522	ESM19	Long	2	-$300	$2,038	$100	UFO	A	Solid Trading, with a focus on making sure I snap a picture of the setups & exits properly.	
20190522	ESM19	Long	2	-$225	$1,925	$100	UFO	B-	Wasn't sure about placing the trailing stop below ally UFOs, I assumed it has to be placed in white space below ally UFOs on Edge TFs.	5
20190523										2
20190524	ESM19	Long	2	-$500	$1,500	$100	UFO	C+	Trade 1: Very bad risk management.	
20190524	CLN19	Short	2	-$160	$310	$180	UFO	A-	Trade 2: Good trade, managed properly, conserverd profit instead of incurring a loss	3
20190525									Live Q&A session with Jose	3
20190526									Learning Options with Jose	2
20190527	CLN19	Long	2			-$60	UFO	F	Learning Options with Jose while trading	
20190527	CLN19	Long	2			-$40	UFO	F		3
20190528	ESM19	Long	2	-$250	$375	$375	UFO	B-	Trying to refine the Time-In-Trade rule	4
20190529									Learning Options, lots of meetings at work, cant trade	3
20190530	ESM19	Long	2	-$250	$388	$388	UFO	B-	Need to contact Jose about Time-In-Trade rule. Listening to Options with Jose	4

You can use Microsoft Excel, Google Sheets or Apple Numbers, but it is good to use a spreadsheet format – it will make it easier to filter, sort and analyze your trade data.

We are now at the end of the flowchart:

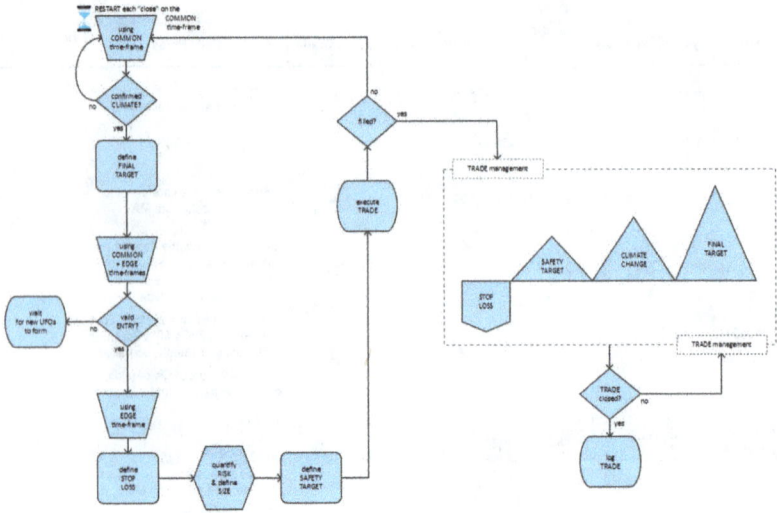

The flowchart summarizes everything we have covered and gives you a step-by-step guide to following the methodology. It would be a good idea to keep this (or something like it) handy as you're analyzing and placing trades.

BEING HUMAN

We started this book talking about trading psychology. It is important that we understand this as it can be the cause for most traders to struggle. Trading is indeed an emotional game that triggers many human emotions that could be powerful – and lethal - at the same time.

Human emotions are often a key cause of problems in Trading, and the more we can be aware of the impact of being human on our trading, the more we can mitigate the downsides.

Most starting Traders fall into the following two traps:

1. Not realizing that the impact of human emotions happens at a subconscious level and feeling that they are in control when the opposite is true.
2. Ignoring the importance of mastering their own Trading psychology, focused only on the Trading method, without embracing the fact that we are all human and therefore vulnerable.

It is very common for a lot of traders when they first enter the world of trading and investing to seek only to gain knowledge and skill. The thought process is, "I'm a smart person, give me a methodology to learn and I'll just apply it."

This is especially true for people who follow processes normally in their lives, such as engineers. It's easy to believe that we can learn a process, execute that process and the results will come.

However, the difference between following a process in a work-place environment and following a trading process for yourself is that you – and only you – click the button when trading, with no one else to hold accountable. You are watching your own money go up and down. To you, the profit or loss means something.

Maybe if you moved your target further away on an investment, that profit would mean paying off the mortgage earlier. Or a few losses in a row could add up to your normal weekly or monthly expenses and responsibilities. These things mean something to us as human beings and we are acting only by ourselves, making decisions for our own trading accounts all the time. No one is telling us what to do, or when or how to do it.

You must be disciplined with your time, your risk and your approach. You must behave consistently.

The markets require us to be objective and rational and, as human beings, we are often not those things. We can use techniques to minimize this impact, such as using one platform for planning and one for execution, using technology to do a lot of analysis for us, and understanding how our plan suits us as individuals BEFORE we trade (i.e., which timeframes, risk tolerance, etc., suit you as a trader).

We need to accept that we are human. We know how to trade, we understand the markets, but we also understand that we are psychological beings. Losses can cause us to feel that we are "losers" or undermine our confidence in what we're doing; it can be hard to see them as simple data collection or something necessary for the sake of an overall profitable week, month or year. This can lead to taking trades in "revenge mode", or taking a break from the markets, or even stepping back from trading entirely. On the other hand, winners can cause us to become overconfident and believe that we are Gods of Trading and we end up potentially risking more or changing where we place targets, etc.

Neither of these are rational or objective ways of approaching trading, but they are very human responses to the realities of trading.

THE UNFORTUNATE PATH

Here is a typical process when a starting Trader gets involved in the Trading business without a proper mindset:

- Acquiring Trading knowledge
- Practice, practice, practice, and excitement

- Collecting profits and losses
- Greed kicking in
- Emotions taking over
- Breaking rules, anger, revenge Trading, etc.
- Lack of consistency
- Giving up or failure

It's important to understand that this is an ugly reality for a lot of traders. Understanding what not to do can help us avoid getting into trouble ourselves.

Of course, we need to acquire trading knowledge and practice it to build a skill. But having knowledge, and even skill, without the proper mindset and self-understanding, is likely to still lead traders down the Unfortunate Path.

In the end, we are the ones running our Trading business and making executive decisions about Trades all the time. Not realizing the importance of Trading psychology – being in denial mode as if it's not an important aspect of Trading, or delaying its understanding by putting our focus exclusively on a Trading methodology – carries an expensive price to pay.

We need to master ourselves as much as we need to master the Markets. The Markets will always be bigger than us and the Markets will always be right and behave unexpectedly. Our job as traders is to be humble, avoid the arrogance of thinking we know it all, manage our risk and discipline ourselves to follow a consistent plan and methodology.

THE ATHLETE WAY

Just like athletes prepare themselves mentally before competing, expert Traders do the same. Professional tennis players behave differently than those who play tennis as a hobby. Both can lead to the individual having fun and being healthier, but the success levels are extremely different.

This is the same in the trading world – you don't need to be the best trader to have some level of success and enjoy what you're doing. As long as you follow rules and have a certain level of skill, you can be good at tennis and, similarly, you can be a good trader. The more professionally you can approach it, the more likely you are to reach greater successes, but it's not essential for you to be in the game.

In the same way professional athletes will have routines before they play to get their focus in the right place, it is also helpful for us as traders to prepare for the game that is trading the financial markets. Developing routines and using tools such as meditation or visualization are common to make sure our mindset is in the right place before we begin Trading.

THE "C" WORD

Most Traders would think that the "C" word is "Consistency". While it is true that the ultimate goal of a Trader is to obtain consistent results, the fact is that none of it can be achieved without consistent action – and consistent action cannot be executed without a proper level of confidence.

Proper practice builds up confidence, but only Traders ready to invest some time and effort can achieve that stage.

It is confidence that allows us to act consistently. Without confidence in our methodology, we wouldn't click the button. We usually get confidence in anything by seeing the results first, but we need to trade in order to see results.

It is helpful to practice using paper money (simulated accounts) and log the results before going to live trading so you can gain not just the experience and skill but, most importantly, the confidence that you will need to continue to enact your methodology consistently.

> Experience tells you what to do;
> **Confidence** allows you to do it.
> Stan Smith

Acknowledgments

Jose: Hey Becky

Becky: Hi Jose

Jose: Thank you Becky

Becky: Thank you Jose

Becky: Feels so good to be able to finally celebrate the fact that our book is finished ... and to finally celebrate it in person...

Jose: Can you believe it? We started before the Covid-19 pandemic and since then, no hugs, no meetings in person...

Becky: True! But a few important things have happened, though! We've got so many people to thank...

Jose: What a couple of years! You've gotten married and I've got a baby daughter born ... and with all of that, the people around us still allowed us to push the book through.

Becky: We're lucky! We're lucky in many ways ... we're lucky to be surrounded by the ones who love us and we're of course lucky to be traders.

Jose: Indeed! So, who do we thank first?

Becky: I would want to thank my wife, Marisi. She supports me in every choice I make and everything I do, bringing me cups of tea whilst I shut myself in a room and worked on the book. I couldn't be more thankful to her. I'd also like to thank both my parents, who acted as sounding boards for me and listened to me talk about the book for countless hours!

Jose: In my case, I'd like to start by thanking Nienie. My wife is just everything in everything I do and I am. I could not get this book done without her and since she was pregnant with Anya for some time while this book was being written, I would also want to thank my daughter for being a source of inspiration, when I think of the future of the new generations who are starting their lives in the present.

Becky: I'm sure Anya will be inspiring people for years to come!

Jose: Thank you, Becky ... so many reasons to be grateful beyond the love and support at home. I am so lucky to have real friends and also colleagues that motivated me in ways which impacted the philosophy behind this book. More specifically my team at Traddictiv is simply the best team one can be part of ... I want to thank you all for that, as you help me be better each day and this is for sure reflected in this book.

Becky: The team we have is amazing; a network of traders and amazing people that I love working with, as well as the students and UFO users who join our sessions and make doing this even more fun.

Jose: I also want to thank our UFO trader friends out there in the world, as we could not be thinking of helping the trader communities the way we do unless we had your support the way I feel it. Thank you!

About the Authors

Jose Blasco is a multi-asset trader who specializes in options, equities, futures and currencies. Since he began trading in 2008, he has accumulated a wealth of knowledge on global markets, trading both directional and non-directional strategies across multiple timeframes. In 2011, he began sharing his expertise as a trading instructor, delivering training in person as well as online and appearing on live broadcast events.

Since 2018, Jose has developed innovative trading technology as the principal of Traddictiv PTE.LTD, where he also mentors traders worldwide. In addition, Jose has served as an engineering professor, tapping into his love of technology to teach online trading techniques. His multilingual skills allow him to travel the world and keep abreast of global markets.

What motivates me:

I just love the markets. I love them all, and I love them with a healthy mix of peace and passion!

As a result, I am always ready to click the button if the market provides me with opportunities that meet my trading rules, and always eager to screen-share and team up when running trading sessions, leading my students to work with me on setups and executions.

I also love technology and the fact that it saves me time and allows me to approach trading objectively, which allows me to enjoy the satisfaction that comes with a job well done.

What I like to trade:

Everything in life has pros and cons – and, in this sense, being a bit of a perfectionist, I like to keep the pros and get rid of the cons by using different trading instruments for different trading purposes.

For instance, my use of Futures is devoted to intra-day trading exclusively, while with Options, Forex or Stocks, I open the door to other trading styles with longer durations as well as being directional and non-directional via combinations of assets.

I like to be properly diversified with different products, different strategies and different time exposures.

Outside of trading:

I have my family on the top of the priority list. The beauty of trading is that market hours and personal time can be made compatible. I am very lucky to have additional passions that my family also enjoys sharing with me.

One of these hobbies is ballroom dancing, which used to be a very intense time of my life during 10 years where I competed actively and even got some professional recognitions, as well as organized official international competitions in my city.

My other little obsession is a bit noisier, as it has to do with motorsports – more specifically, Formula 1, which I have followed since I was a little boy. While regular cars do not interest me that much, I travel to F1 tracks on a regular basis, enjoy the competition and if possible, take some driving lessons in such circuits.

Becky Hayman has been in the markets since 2013, with particular experience in the Forex and Futures markets. She specializes mainly in trade plans and back-testing, helping traders build their own unique trading plans and understand how to test them effectively and efficiently.

Having worked in education for multiple years, from teaching classes to one-on-one coaching, Becky is passionate about the learning process for students of trading.

A passion to travel fuels her love for the financial markets and she hopes to use her experience to help others shorten their learning curves and achieve their own goals efficiently.

What motivates me:

I am particularly motivated to help shorten the learning curve for other traders and help them get to confidence with their strategy sooner. Like many traders, I've tried multiple approaches and seemed to be hitting a brick wall a lot. I know this happens with many who try trading and I want to help them to find their way around the wall.

What I like to trade:

I have been trading FX and Futures for years. FX particularly suits me as I like to swing trade, which allows me to have more time flexibility around my trading and allows me to travel more without worrying so much about missing opportunities. I like being able to use technology that I can apply to any currency pair.

Outside of trading:

I absolutely love to travel. Covid notwithstanding, I usually take around six to eight trips a year, whether that's a short weekend break to a European city or a big trip of a few weeks to somewhere exotic in Southeast Asia, South America or Africa. What I love about trading is that as long as I have internet access, I can look at the markets. One time I was on a train between Oslo and Stockholm, snow-capped mountains and beautiful scenery flying past my window, and an FX chart in front of me. For me, perfect!

Resources

With the purchase of this book, you have unlocked a free Forex course, as well as free access to our AutoClimate™ and AutoUFOs® apps for TradingView for 3 months:

To claim your free Forex course and apps, go to www.tradewithufos.com/redeem

Learning to trade an asset class alone can be difficult and overwhelming. We're here to help you with whatever tools make the most sense for you:

Apps

Apart from using our apps to increase precision trading, AutoClimate™ and AutoUFOs® can be a useful time-saving tool during the learning process, especially when combined with the market replay functionality available in TradingView.

Three links to remember:

Unlocking your free Forex course automatically grants you access to the AutoClimate™ and AutoUFOs® apps for TradingView. www.tradewithufos.com/redeem

TradingView offers a free plan as well as paid memberships (our app works perfectly with their free plan). Start your own TradingView account here:
www.tradewithufos.com/tradingview

Explore other trading apps, such as the MetaTrader apps, right here:
www.tradewithufos.com/apps

Coaching

The knowledge acquired by reading this book provides a great foundation. In general, we cannot do much without knowledge – congratulations for being open to educating yourself!

Having said that, experience proves that knowledge is step one, which should be followed by step two, which is skill building through practice. Here are additional free resources to eliminate bad habits that come from isolation and help transform your knowledge into a powerful skill:

Attend live trading and coaching sessions. Interact with your coach and other traders. Ask questions. www.tradewithufos.com/coaching

Watch recorded trading and coaching sessions to save time and speed up your development:
www.youtube.com/c/tradewithufos

Additional Courses

One of the risks attached to trading is falling in love with trading, as many of us do. Now that you have learned a lot about Forex trading, you may realize that you'd like to work further on your trading plan, maybe you'd prefer to refine your methodology using back-testing techniques, or you now understand the impact of trading emotions and you'd like to work further on mastering the trader in you, or you'd simply like to learn to trade other assets, such as stocks, options, futures or digital/crypto assets.

To help you understand your education choices further go to: www.tradewithufos.com/courses

FAQ

We expect you to have questions while going through the process of learning how to trade or working to improve your current skillset. If you have any questions, please feel free to use the Q&A section on our website. You can also connect with Jose and Becky there: www.tradewithufos.com/questions

Social Media and Contact

We are online and we love interaction!

Please find us on your favorite social media network, or use our support email: support@traddictiv.com

Our social media channels are all here: https://linktr.ee/tradewithufos

We would truly appreciate if you could follow/like us – and, most importantly, share the word with the world! Many people may be able to use our help. They just need to know we exist ☺

Thank you for reading us!

Glossary

Ally UFO = Existing UFOs which are compatible with the trade direction – i.e., buy UFOs if your position is long or sell UFOs if your position is short (UFOs are plotted on the charts using the AutoUFOs® app).

Ask = Price set by the sellers, where sellers' limit orders are waiting to be filled. A market buy order would have to buy from the Ask price.

Base vs Quote = The base is first currency shown in a Forex Currency Pair (e.g. "EUR" in "EURUSD"). The quote is the second currency shown in a Forex Currency Pair (e.g. "USD" in "EURUSD"). Together, the Currency Pair indicate how much quote currency is needed to buy one unit of the base currency. (e.g. "EURUSD = 1.55" means $1.55 (USD) is needed to purchase one euro.

Bid = Price set by buyers, where buyers' limit orders are waiting to be filled. A market sell order would have to sell to the Bid price.

Bid/Ask Spread (or Spread) = The difference between the Bid and Ask price.

Broker = The company who sends your buy and sell orders to the exchange or interbank market.

Buy Order = An instruction to your broker to buy the base currency (and therefore sell the quote currency).

Candle (or Bar) = The graphical elements on a chart that represent price movement for a given time period.

Currency Pair = A quotation of the value of one currency versus one other. (e.g., EURUSD is the Euro versus the US Dollar).

Entry = Initiating a trade (or adding more to an existing position) by buying (long) or selling (short).

Exotic Currency Pairs = Thinly traded currency pairs that are not widely used in global transactions, e.g., USDSEK (US Dollar/Swedish Krona), GBPMXN (Great British Pound/Mexican Peso), etc.

Filled Order = A buy and sell transaction of an equal size and price taking place, e.g., one lot of EURUSD being "filled" means there was one lot being bought and sold at the same price.

Fundamental Analysis = Methods that attempt to measure the intrinsic value of an instrument by reviewing factors such as political, economic and social influences.

Last = The price at which the last transaction took place (either buyers bought at the Ask or sellers sold to the Bid).

Leverage = A multiplier effect as a consequence of trading on margin, otherwise understood as a ratio of the trader's funds to the size of the trade allowed to be executed by their broker.

Limit Order = An order to buy or sell only if the market reaches a pre-defined price (or better).

Liquidity = The likelihood of finding a counterparty to fill our orders – e.g., finding a buyer for a sell order or a seller for a buy order.

Long = Entering a position by buying. Profit is realized if the instrument rises in value. In Forex trading, going long means buying and expecting the base currency to appreciate against the quote currency.

Lots = Refers to the size of the trade (the amount of currency used). A Standard lot is worth 100,000 of the base currency.

Major Currency Pairs = The most liquid currency pairs in the world (and they are all connected to the US dollar – e.g., EURUSD, AUDUSD, etc.).

Margin = Capital required by brokers to be allowed to execute a trade of a specific size.

Margin Call = The broker's demand that an investor deposits additional money or securities so that the account is brought up to the minimum value to maintain trade positions.

Market Climate = The statistical definition of a market condition that includes direction/trend of a market and duration (plotted on the charts using the AutoClimate™ app).

Market Order = An order to buy or sell an instrument at the current market price.

Micro-Lots = Refers to the size of the trade. A Micro-Lot is worth 1,000 of the base currency.

Mini-Lots = Refers to the size of the trade. A Mini-Lot is worth 10,000 of the base currency.

Minors (Or Cross Pairs) = Currency pairs that have lower liquidity than majors but are still liquid enough markets. (Although this list can contain US Dollar pairs – e.g., USDSGD – this list often contains combinations of highly liquid currencies that do not contain the US Dollar (e.g., EURAUD, GBPCAD, NZDJPY, etc.).

OTC = Over-The-Counter.

Pip = Stands for Percentage in Point and refers to the minimum price fluctuation in a currency pair.

Pip Value = How much each Pip is worth when traded with one micro-lot.

Platform = The software/interface that you use to view charts, see the pricing matrix, apply indicators, plan and execute your trades, etc.

Reward = How much your trade can profit.

Reward-To-Risk Ratio = The average profit you make when your trades achieve a profitable result versus the average loss you take when your trades produce losses.

Risk = How much your trade can lose.

Rival UFO = Existing UFOs which are contrary to the trade direction – i.e., sell UFOs if your position is long or buy UFOs if your position is short (UFOs are plotted on the charts using the AutoUFOs® app).

Rollover = A process run by Forex brokers to continuously push settlement dates back in time.

Sell Order = An instruction to your broker to sell the base currency (and therefore buy the quote currency).

Short = Entering a position by selling. Profit is realized if the instrument decreases in value. In Forex trading, going short means selling and expecting the base currency to depreciate against the quote currency.

Slippage = Being filled at a worse price than expected – e.g., buying higher than anticipated or selling lower than anticipated.

Stop Loss = Programmed orders that take you out of a losing position automatically, even if you are not watching your screen, or have no access to your trading platforms.

Swap = An interest rate differential between two currency pairs that is created by the rollover process.

Target = Where (at what price) you will get out of the trade if you were to profit.

Technical Analysis = Methods that attempt to forecast future price movements of an instrument based on historical price movements and patterns.

Technical Indicators (or Studies) = Computational analysis techniques, typically plotted on price charts automatically and used by traders to help predict future price movements based on technical information such as price and volume.

Timeframe = The lifespan of each candle/bar on a chart – e.g., a four-hour timeframe means each candle/bar represents four hours' worth of trading data.

Un-Filled Order = Orders that are still waiting to be executed or cancelled (have not been filled yet).

Volatility = The speed of price movement or how far price moves within given periods of time.

Volume = The number of units traded in a market.

Win/Loss Ratio = The number of winners out of the trades you take (e.g., 30% win/loss ratio = 30% of the trades you executed are profitable).